MEMOIRS OF A
FLYING TIGER

The Story of a WWII Veteran and SIA Pioneer Pilot

MEMOIRS OF A
FLYING TIGER

The Story of a WWII Veteran and SIA Pioneer Pilot

Captain Ho Weng Toh

with Jonathan Y. H. Sim

World Scientific

NEW JERSEY · LONDON · SINGAPORE · BEIJING · SHANGHAI · HONG KONG · TAIPEI · CHENNAI · TOKYO

Published by

World Scientific Publishing Co. Pte. Ltd.
5 Toh Tuck Link, Singapore 596224
USA office: 27 Warren Street, Suite 401-402, Hackensack, NJ 07601
UK office: 57 Shelton Street, Covent Garden, London WC2H 9HE

British Library Cataloguing-in-Publication Data
A catalogue record for this book is available from the British Library.

MEMOIRS OF A FLYING TIGER
The Story of a WWII Veteran and SIA Pioneer Pilot

Copyright © 2020 by World Scientific Publishing Co. Pte. Ltd.

All rights reserved. This book, or parts thereof, may not be reproduced in any form or by any means, electronic or mechanical, including photocopying, recording or any information storage and retrieval system now known or to be invented, without written permission from the publisher.

For photocopying of material in this volume, please pay a copying fee through the Copyright Clearance Center, Inc., 222 Rosewood Drive, Danvers, MA 01923, USA. In this case permission to photocopy is not required from the publisher.

ISBN 978-981-120-543-9
ISBN 978-981-120-643-6 (pbk)

For any available supplementary material, please visit
https://www.worldscientific.com/worldscibooks/10.1142/11417#t=suppl

Desk Editor: Sandhya Venkatesh

Typeset by Stallion Press
Email: enquiries@stallionpress.com

Printed in Singapore

FOREWORD

I thank my 99 year-old friend, Captain Ho Weng Toh and his son, Fred Ho, for giving me the privilege of writing the foreword of this inspiring book. Many of Captain Ho's friends have been urging him for many years to write his memoirs. I am glad that he has done so, with the help of Jonathan Y.H. Sim.

What lessons have I learnt from reading Captain Ho's memoirs?

First, I learn that life is full of unexpected twists and turns. Captain Ho never set out to be a pilot. After finishing his high school in Ipoh, a town in the state of Perak in Malaysia, he went to further his studies in Hong Kong in 1941. The British had established Hong Kong University in 1911, many years before the University of Malaya was founded. Captain Ho wanted to study engineering at Hong Kong University. However, he couldn't get into the Faculty of Engineering and was offered a place in the Science Faculty.

In December 1941, Hong Kong was invaded and occupied by Japan. With a group of his school mates, Captain Ho managed to escape from occupied Hong Kong to free China. Whilst living in a small town called Pingshi, in the Guangdong province, and studying at the Sun Yat-Sen University, Captain Ho saw an advertisement, in the local newspaper, calling for applicants to be trained as pilots of the new China Air Force. The old China Air Force had been destroyed by Japan. He applied and was accepted.

Second, I learn that Captain Ho was an accidental war hero. He never intended to be a combat pilot. To qualify as a military pilot, Captain Ho underwent training in China, India (Lahore) and United States. On his return to China, he was a member of the famous Flying Tigers, the new China Air Force, established with the help of US Air Force General, Claire Chennault. Captain Ho was a bomber pilot. He flew several bombing missions against the Japanese Army and, miraculously, survived. Many of his friends were not so lucky and never returned from their missions.

Third, I learn that Captain Ho was one of the pilots who helped to establish Singapore Airline, after the breakup of Malaya Singapore Airline. Captain Ho was one of SIA's senior pilots and the Chief Pilot of SIA's B737 fleet. He was asked to be an instructor. He succeeded in training about many pilots for SIA. Captain Ho was not only a teacher but also a role model for and a mentor to many young pilots. They loved and respected him and gave him a nickname, "Daddy O". SIA should never forget the debt it owes to Captain Ho and other pioneer pilots.

Fourth, I learn that Captain Ho was a very good leader. Captain Ho believes that a leader should be humble and considerate towards his subordinates. He believes in the saying: "You cannot demand respect. You command respect by respecting others." He believes that kindness and humility are the key qualities of a good leader. Captain walked his talk as he had always treated his subordinates and both the flight crew and ground crew with respect and kindness. We need more leaders like him.

It has been a privilege knowing Captain Ho Weng Toh. I hope his book will inspire many young Singaporeans.

Tommy Koh
Professor of Law, NUS
Ambassador-At-Large, MFA

FOREWORD

by George Yeo

It has been my good fortune to know Captain Ho Weng Toh in the last seven years. While in Government, I had not heard of him. In my nine years as Minister for Information and the Arts, when part of my responsibility was to promote Singapore's heritage, his name never surfaced as an important figure in Singapore's history. Yet, on the 70th anniversary of the end of the Second World War in 2015, he, as a Singapore citizen, was honored both in Beijing and in Taipei for his contribution to the anti-Japanese war effort, one of the few surviving members of the Flying Tigers.

Captain Ho was largely forgotten in Singapore because he did not fit neatly into our national narrative. He grew up in Ipoh. It was from Japanese-occupied Hong Kong that he escaped into Kuomintang (KMT) China and subsequently joined the China Air Force. He identified with China as his ancestral motherland and, while holding a Nationalist Chinese passport, learned to fly in British India and the US. When the civil war between the KMT and the Communists resumed in China after the end of the Second World War, he opted out from a combat role and subsequently returned to British Malaya where he chafed at being classified as a 'British protected subject'. Some years later, he decided that his entire family should register themselves as Singapore citizens under the Lim Yew Hock government.

By any measure, Captain Ho was a hero. He did not set out to be one. As an undergraduate in Hong Kong University, he took great risks to help fellow students who were interned in Sham Shui Po. At that time, he could see Kai Tak Airport from May Hall. His escape from Hong Kong to Kukong (Shaoguan) in 1942, at that time still under KMT control, was gripping.

He was determined to become a combat pilot and admitted to great satisfaction strafing and killing Japanese soldiers on his second bombing mission in northern China. "Each time I opened up the machine guns to fire at them, I told myself that this was for all the cruel and evil things they had done to China and to my compatriots. This was payback for all the horrible and wicked things — the rape, the torture, the murder — that they had done to my friends back in Hong Kong, and to everyone else in China." Many in the Flying Tigers died during the war. He was sometimes fearful but never allowed that fear to overcome him.

Captain Ho's autobiography is written with unaffected modesty and humility. He wrote as if the things he did were things anyone would or could have done. He recalled his relationship with girl friends in Malaya, the US, China and Hong Kong in a touching manner but without an excess of emotion. That is only reserved for his wife who bore him two sons and a daughter, and died too young from cancer.

In his youth, he never imagined himself becoming a pilot. Flying became a passion. He found a vocation in training and mentoring young pilots. Among older Singapore Airlines pilots, he was fondly called 'daddy-o'. While flying in Malayan Airlines during colonial times, he and other local pilots resented the racial discrimination.

I got to know Captain Ho because of my association with Robert Kuok. One day, through an intermediary, I received a message requesting me to put him in touch with Robert Kuok in Hong Kong. After Singapore's separation from Malaysia in 1965, Malaysian Airways became Malaysia-Singapore Airlines. Dr Goh Keng Swee proposed Robert Kuok, a Malaysian with business connections to Singapore, as Chairman to Malaysian Prime Minister Tunku Abdul Rahman. Captain Ho was then the Chief Pilot. Robert Kuok was delighted to meet Captain Ho again after many years and hosted him to a nostalgic dinner at Hong Kong Island Shangri-La. I was spellbound by Captain Ho's stories that evening and encouraged him to write his autobiography. It was assuming how Robert Kuok kept addressing him 'Uncle Ho' saying that it made him feel young.

Captain Ho is remarkably fit and erect at 99. A few years ago, we met for breakfast at the Botanic Garden. He had taken a wrong turning and was just a little flustered. I was unnecessarily concerned for him. He commented drily that "I can't believe how old I am". He was then 95. Last year, he could not come for my Chinese New Year open house because of a fall. Somehow I was not too worried. True enough, he was up and about again after a few weeks.

He walks everyday from his flat in Pasir Ris to a nearby park for his daily exercise. He continues to keep a wide circle of old and young friends. Last year, I introduced him to Mothership.Sg which did a couple of uplifting pieces on his remarkable life. In the epilogue to his book, he emphasized the importance of loving and serving. His positive spirit is an inspiration. His short autobiography is a gem.

DEDICATION

This book is dedicated to my beloved late father, Ho Kok Lim and mother Chow Keng Sin and dear wife Augusta.

CONTENTS

Foreword   v
by Tommy Koh

Foreword   ix
by George Yeo

Dedication   xiii

Chapter 1	Morning has Broken	1
Chapter 2	A Christmas Wish	7
Chapter 3	Meaningfully Occupied	13
Chapter 4	A Harrowing Journey	19
Chapter 5	Struggle	33
Chapter 6	The Door of Destiny	41
Chapter 7	A New Life	45
Chapter 8	Spreading My Wings	55
Chapter 9	They Called Me Winkie	59
Chapter 10	Flying Solo	63
Chapter 11	Friends Coming and Going	69
Chapter 12	Sad Departure	79
Chapter 13	Troubled Waters	89

Chapter 14	Mission Accomplished	93
Chapter 15	Civil War	107
Chapter 16	The Gift	113
Chapter 17	One Love Gained, One Love Lost	119
Chapter 18	Flight of Refuge	129
Chapter 19	A Revolutionary Change	135
Chapter 20	To Greener Pastures	143
Chapter 21	Embracing New Identities	157
Chapter 22	Paving the Way with Hardship	167
Chapter 23	Daddy-O	177
Chapter 24	A Student Once Again	187
Chapter 25	Turbulence	195
Chapter 26	Many Happy Landings	209

Epilogue 211

Photos 215

Chapter 1

MORNING HAS BROKEN

Monday, 8 December 1941

May Hall, Hong Kong University

Days away from the final examinations, I had been up since the break of dawn, studying in the cosy confines of my room. My eyes had grown weary from hours of reading, but I was determined not to stop at all cost.

I finally fulfilled my long-time aspiration to study at the prestigious Hong Kong University (HKU). I was given a private room in May Hall, a very beautiful and grand, three-storey red brick hostel run by the University. Much more than that, I was very fortunate to be assigned a 'boy' who would attend to my needs. He would make my bed, serve my meals, polish my shoes and run errands on my behalf. He was a valet in the true British colonial tradition.

In the common room of May Hall, there were drinks, radios, card games, and many other forms of entertainment that can keep a young man occupied in his leisure time. These were provided to facilitate interactions between students from various backgrounds. We have had many festive gatherings and parties here.

Life has finally been so good to me. I had made it after two long and arduous years of struggle since the day I left my hometown in Ipoh, Malaya (present day Malaysia). I had made it this far. I certainly did not want to lose it all from being complacent.

* * *

Looking back, when I was a teenager, I long aspired to become an engineer. But to realise this aspiration, I had to go abroad for further studies. HKU was, and still is, one of the most pre-eminent universities in Asia. With that aspiration set firmly in my heart, I left home at the age of 19, for the very first time in June 1939, and made my voyage by ship to Hong Kong (via Singapore).

When I finally arrived in Hong Kong, I was quite disappointed to learn that my Senior Cambridge results were not enough to qualify for HKU. Instead, I had to find an institution that could prepare me for matriculation into HKU. I discovered that my qualifications sufficed for admissions into St. Stephen's College. So, I enrolled and began my matriculation studies there. But I had a difficult time adjusting to the culture, as it was a school for children of aristocrats and political elites. After one term, I left the college and decided that it might be better if I studied for the matriculation exams on my own.

Around the same time, I discovered that I was eligible to pursue my studies at Lingnan University, a private university started in 1888 by a group of American missionaries in Guangzhou. But due to the Sino-Japanese War in China, the missionaries moved the campus to Hong Kong. I enrolled into the university as a backup plan. If I couldn't pass my matriculation exams to study at HKU, I could at least complete my studies at Lingnan.

Lessons at Lingnan were held at night, as it shared the same campus with HKU (which conducted lessons in the day). Moreover, lessons were taught in Chinese. Like many of the overseas Chinese students, I struggled with the Chinese language, due to my many years of English education at St. Michael's Institution, a Christian mission school back in Ipoh. The University was well aware that there were many overseas Chinese students like me, and they held special foundational Chinese classes for us. While I appreciated the classes, this meant that I had significantly less time to spare.

By day, I was busy studying for HKU's matriculation exams. By night, I was busy studying engineering and the Chinese language at Lingnan. This made it incredibly difficult for me to spend time with any of the friends I knew in Hong Kong. There was no time for a social life. It was a difficult and an incredibly lonely time.

In June 1940, I received my matriculation results. My results were not good enough to pursue engineering at HKU, but I nonetheless qualified to pursue the Sciences. Though I was a bit disappointed, I was largely overjoyed to receive the results. I passed and cleared my first major hurdle since leaving home. I finally gained admission into HKU!

In September 1940, I commenced my first semester at HKU. While I was indeed elated to finally study at the University of my dreams, my first year of studies was anything but a bed of roses. I had to major in Physics, Chemistry, and Mathematics, which happened to be my weakest subjects. As there were only ten of us who pursued this academic route, we attracted the individual attention of our lecturers, who were determined to work us as hard as they could. That particular year was extremely tough for me. I had chosen to concentrate on Mathematics and Physics, as these were my weakest subjects. Yet, I held the hope of transferring to the Engineering faculty.

Despite my sweat and struggle over an entire year, my grades were poor, and I could not make the transfer. Realising that the pursuit of engineering would be nothing more than flogging a dead horse, I switched to the Arts Faculty in my second year. This was something I was most proficient in, as my education back in Ipoh had prepared me very well for it.

* * *

It was slightly past 8 o'clock in the morning. I was determined not to let the fatigue of studying affect me. After a two-year long struggle, it seemed that I had reached a turning point in my life. Since the arts were relatively easy for me, I was confident of graduating with flying colours. A promising future was awaiting me.

All of a sudden, I heard a loud noise coming from outside. Before I was able to make sense of what was going on, the intensity of the noise increased.

BOOM! BOOM! BOOM!

The sounds resounded loudly in quick succession.

BOOM! BOOM! BOOM!

My desk was shaking. I felt the walls vibrate too.

BOOM! BOOM! BOOM!

There was a lot of commotion outside. People were screaming. There were people shouting as well. But I was unable to make out what they were saying. I was in a daze.

What was happening?

I rushed out of my room to the balcony just outside to investigate. From the balcony, I had a clear view of the Kai Tak Airport, which was about 15 miles away. The airport had always been a pleasant sight for me. That day, it was not.

Above the airport were plumes of black smoke rising up to the sky.

I was confused by what I saw. From a distance, I could faintly see what looked like bomber planes circling above the airport. Wherever those planes went, they left a trail of thick black smoke rising from the ground below.

I was terrified.

The sound of explosions were awfully clear to me. So too were the screams of fear and anguish.

Overwhelmed and horrified, I took a step back and closed the balcony window. This was too much for me.

I quickly switched on the radio, hoping to hear an explanation that could make sense of what I had just witnessed.

In a deep solemn voice, the radio announcer said, "The war is on. The Japanese are here."

Chapter 2

A CHRISTMAS WISH

Wednesday, 24 December 1941

It's Christmas Eve, but the atmosphere was far from festive. Many students, including myself, had been hiding in May Hall since the Japanese first launched an attack on Hong Kong. For two weeks, we had been hearing the whistling sounds of artillery shells raining from the sky, followed by the sounds of the explosions. There was no respite, not even for a brief moment.

None of us dared to leave the safe refuge of May Hall. What if we got hit by the artillery fire or by a piece of stray shrapnel from the explosion? We didn't want to die. We were very afraid.

Many of us were just wishing for a Christmas miracle.

* * *

In the months prior to the invasion, we had heard about the unimaginable horrors of what the Japanese did to the people of China during the Sino-Japanese War of 1937 and the "Rape of Nanking" in 1938, which resulted in the massacre of about 300,000 prisoners of war, innocent refugees and civilians. We knew that it was not long before Hong Kong would fall into their hands.

Since the attack on the Kai Tak Airport, the Japanese invasion into Hong Kong had been swift. In a couple of hours, the Northern parts of Hong Kong — the New Territories and Kowloon — fell into the hands of Japanese. All that's left was the island of Hong Kong itself.

Though Hong Kong island was heavily defended, the British had grossly miscalculated that an invasion would come from the South. They did not expect an invasion coming from the North at all. For two weeks, the British persisted in defending the island. Fighting has been intense, and the Japanese certainly didn't look like they were going to give up.

Now that Hong Kong was faced with the Japanese threat, we could not help but wonder if the British would continue to protect us. Or would they flee and leave us to fend for ourselves? What was most worrisome of all was the complete silence from the Government House.

Peeking out through the windows, all we saw were plumes of black smoke rising up into the sky. All our hopes, our aspirations, our dreams had since gone up in smoke too. Filling up the void within us was a sense of dread and anxiety. It felt like there was no escape. Over the radio, we heard news that the Japanese had conquered other parts of Asia. There was nowhere to run. There was nowhere to hide. The Japanese were everywhere.

It was either death, or a life of misery that awaited us all.

* * *

Thursday, 25 December 1941

It was Christmas Day. We had grown so accustomed to the incessant sounds of artillery fire, that the unusual silence was so deafening. It was as if the invasion had stopped. Yet, none of us were sure whether we should celebrate this change of events.

Did our Christmas wish come true?

By about 4 o'clock in the afternoon, a commotion broke out outside. It was anything but merry.

The British had surrendered.

* * *

Not long after the announcement of surrender, the victorious Japanese troops began rounding up prisoners-of-war (POWs) all over the Hong Kong island. Anyone found wearing a military uniform was rounded up and forced to join a long march of POWs toward an internment camp.

I didn't know what possessed me, but when I heard this, I left the safety of May Hall to observe the march of the captives. Amongst the numerous POWs that had been rounded up were many young boys, who were around the age of 18–19 years old, dressed in military uniforms. I recognised many of their faces! In fact, some of them were my friends! They weren't soldiers at all. Rather, they were medical students of Hong Kong University (HKU)!

Months before the surrender, Professor Lindsay Ride, the respected Dean of Medicine at HKU (and a colonel of the British Army), persuaded his first- and second-year medical students to join the Red Cross Medical Relief Corps, so as to form a medical unit in the event of an emergency. He promised those who signed up that they would be granted an academic advantage. These student volunteers had to attend weekend courses in first aid and weapons handling, and they were issued military uniforms and guns for their own protection if they ever had to go out searching for injured people.

This seemed like a really good deal. Not only would they get good grades, but they were also given the chance to play with guns and participate in activities they would not otherwise have experienced. Few thought about the potential risks of signing up. Consequently, a large number of medical students joined, many of whom were from Malaya and Singapore. These students had no idea what they were signing up for.

As I watched the march of the captives, I observed how some of the student-prisoners took advantage of the surrounding crowds to slip away into the mass of curious bystanders, hide in the nearby toilets and come out dressed in civilian attire. These were the few lucky ones who managed to escape.

But there were many others who were unable to slip away. Out of sympathy, I followed the march all the way to a large military camp in Sham Shui Po (meaning, "Deep Water Area"). It was a very large camp, the size of a small town, and even from a distance, it had a very intimidating appearance. I could not imagine the kinds of suffering these student-prisoners had to go through in there.

* * *

That Christmas evening, I returned to my room in May Hall, only to encounter the Japanese up close for the very first time. They had come to hostels in HKU to search for POWs who had escaped.

For years, the fearsome reputation of the Japanese made me anticipate facing a ferocious enemy. Yet, what I encountered were soldiers who looked very ordinary. If not for their uniforms, I would have mistaken them for an average person on the street. It was a peculiar encounter, but one that made me realise how I should not be afraid of them.

Thankfully for me and my housemates, our Christmas evening ended without any incident. What a day!

Chapter 3

MEANINGFULLY OCCUPIED

Over the next few days, the first wave of Japanese soldiers came to Hong Kong island. These were combat troops that were engaged in fighting and killing enemy soldiers on the front lines. Having fought in battle, they had become incapable of differentiating hostiles from innocent civilians. They treated everyone roughly. And if anyone attempted to resist them, or if anyone failed to bow to them in respect, these soldiers did not hesitate to employ the cruellest forms of violence without mercy.

Punishments were metted out with utmost cruelty. Those caught for petty crimes were tied to poles at the jetty during low tide and made to suffer a slow and agonising death as the tides rose slowly over the course of the day. When the high tide was over, all that was left were corpses hanging dry for all of Hong Kong to see.

For those of us who resided in May Hall, we were quite fortunate not to have any contact with these first wave of troops. May Hall was located mid-way up the hills, far from the city areas where these troops were deployed. We heard countless horrific stories. Some of us had the misfortune of witnessing shocking atrocities before our very eyes. We were afraid to leave the hostel. There was no certainty that we would return if we walked out the door. We could be shot, stabbed with a bayonet, or be subjected to some form of sadistic torture and left to die on the streets. We left the refuge of May Hall only when necessary.

The second wave of troops arrived some time later. They were more intelligent and civilised than the first wave. They understood the prestige of Hong Kong University (HKU) and sought to befriend us. In their hopes to win us over, they appointed a highly educated commander, a colonel in the medical corps, to take over the administration of HKU.

One evening, together with a few soldiers, the colonel organised a social evening with piano and song recitals for students residing at the HKU hostels. He was very fluent in the English language. He did his best to ease our anxieties, and made our lives a little easier than it might have otherwise been.

For starters, he allowed us to continue residing in our hostels, and we were provided with shelter, water, electricity, and food (though our diet now consisted mainly of soya beans). This was not great, but it was certainly better than what everyone else in Hong Kong had to go through. I was pleasantly surprised by the arrangement. As an overseas student, I had nowhere else to go if I were kicked out of the hostel.

As HKU was renowned for its Faculty of Medicine, the second thing the colonel did was to offer students jobs as assistants in administering medical services. The job was easy and it didn't require any special expertise. It paid well (HKD$60 per assignment) and it provided us with some money to buy food. Yet, it was extremely difficult deciding whether or not to work for them. Once you accepted the job, you were despised by the locals for behaving like a dog for the Japanese. In the end, many of us accepted the job, not for the sake of the money, but because we believed it was better that we handled our fellow Chinese than have a Japanese soldier mishandle them. This was the least we could do to help our own people.

The mission was simple: we had to help prevent an epidemic outbreak. And we were tasked to visit various districts to inoculate the local people from cholera. At the time, it puzzled me how the enemy was concerned with humanitarian work. It seemed like a contradiction. But at least the work kept us meaningfully occupied, and it afforded us 'protection' from Japanese abuses during this frightening period.

On each trip, we were accompanied by two soldiers. One handled security, while the other issued a vaccination certificate. As students, we were required to interact with the poorest people on the island, such as slum dwellers and the homeless, and to inoculate them. At times, we were stationed at the ferry terminals, and we would look for those who did not have a vaccination certification and coax them to allow us to carry out the inoculation on them.

Though I had no medical knowledge, I learnt how to carry out the task of inoculation well. It turned out to be quite easy to perform. The hard part was having to deal with the insults from my fellow Chinese, who would run us down for being a turncoat or a lackey for the enemy. Not only did they resent the injection, but they were also highly suspicious of it, as they had heard so many rumours of Japanese atrocities in China. Understandably, this made them nervous. Who could blame them? We had to persuade them that their fears were unfounded. But there is only so much we could do to alleviate their fears. After all, the local people were more afraid of the soldiers than they were of the injection.

* * *

With the money earned from administering medical services, I discreetly purchased canned foods and tried to smuggle them into the prisoners-of-war (POW) internment camp at Sham Sui Poh. Some of my HKU friends had been imprisoned there simply because they were caught wearing military uniforms for the Red Cross Medical

Relief Corps. Given how the day-to-day life of an ordinary citizen was already quite bad, I imagined how much worse it would have been for my imprisoned friends. I was determined to help them in whatever way I could.

The internment camp was surrounded with barbed wire fences, manned by machine-gunners in watch towers, and patrolled by guards with attack dogs to deter any would-be escapees. Using the darkness of night as my cover, I played hide and seek with the Japanese guards, sneaking through the bushes until I got to a fence. I left the cans of food next to the fence and made my way up to a safe distance, where I used the flag signals I learnt as a Boy Scout to give directions on where they could find the cans of food. It wasn't much, but I could only hope that my friends found the food.

What I did was incredibly risky and foolhardy. Had the Japanese caught me I would certainly have been tortured or shot! But at that time, I thought nothing of the possible consequences. I simply wanted to help my friends.

Unfortunately, after several weeks, I had to stop this dangerous routine as I could not afford enough to sustain myself. All I could do thereafter was to hope and pray for the well-being of my imprisoned friends.

* * *

During the early period of the Japanese occupation of Hong Kong I helped many people, though this often meant putting my own life in danger. Despite the grave risks to my life, my heart gave way each time I encountered people who desperately needed my assistance.

One occasion that left a lasting memory was when I paid a visit to my friend, Florence Wong. She was a resident of Hong Kong and a fellow classmate at HKU. She originally lived in Kowloon with her parents. But when the Japanese invaded Kowloon, her parents sent her and her three siblings away to Hong Kong island, under the care and guardianship of their family maid, with the hope that they would be safe there. It had been some time since I last met her, and I thought it was a good idea to see how she and her siblings were getting along without their parents.

When I reached their apartment in Happy Valley, I was surprised to see that the area was occupied by a contingent of Japanese cavalry. Undeterred, I knocked on the door of her apartment only to find Florence and her siblings crying loudly in distress. Earlier, the soldiers had suddenly barged into their home and forcefully dragged the maid away, where she was raped, tortured, and murdered.

Never before had the reality of death been so profound till this very moment when someone so close had been snatched away from their grasp. Florence and her siblings were incredibly fearful for their lives, and they could not stop crying.

I was at a loss as to how I could help them. I didn't have a place of my own to provide safe refuge. Out of desperation, I thought of the Auw family. They were an Indonesian Chinese family I first encountered on a voyage back to Ipoh, just before I commenced my studies at HKU. They were very kind to me, and when I returned to Hong Kong, I became very good friends with them, and visited their home almost every weekend. They lived in an apartment across the hill at Sun Hui Road (now Caroline Hill Road) in Causeway Bay. And they had a large household of nine persons (including two maids). I realised it would be extremely difficult for them to accommodate another four more persons in their apartment, not to mention providing extra food under such conditions of privation.

Nonetheless, I tried my luck anyway. I phoned the Auw family and asked them if they could accommodate Florence and her siblings. And without hesitation, they were more than happy to accept them into their home. Even if they had to sleep on the floor, they would at least be safe. I was impressed by just how kind and compassionate the Auw family was, and I set out immediately to smuggle the four of them out of their besieged apartment in Happy Valley to the Auw family's abode.

The task was extremely difficult. Four were just too many, and it would have caught the attention of the Japanese. So I had to smuggle them out in pairs. On each trip, we passed over Wong Chou Chung Road, trekked over Caroline Hill, and scurried along Sun Hui Road to the Auw's family apartment. Every moment along the way, we had to be extremely careful not to make a sound or do anything unusual that might attract attention. Along the way, Florence's youngest brother, Henry, was so fearful of being caught that he urinated in his pants!

We were fortunate that both trips went smoothly without a hitch. The four children remained with the Auw family until things settled down under the Japanese occupation.

Weeks later, when the Japanese finally restored telephone services in Hong Kong, Florence phoned her parents in Kowloon, to inform them of what had happened. To her surprise (and mine), her parents knew the Auw family. Florence's parents were so relieved to learn that their children were in the safe hands of a family they could trust.

Chapter 4

A HARROWING JOURNEY

5 August 1942

May Hall, Hong Kong University

I got up very early in the morning, long before the break of dawn. Everyone else in May Hall was still deep in slumber. I, on the other hand, was wide awake, thrilled yet anxious as to what I would do later in the day. Apart from the people involved, no one else had a clue.

I packed my valuables, whatever little I could carry with me: money, precious books, and a few other necessities. The whole time, I tried my best to be as silent and discreet as possible, so as not to wake anyone.

It was about time, and thankfully, I was done packing. All that was left to do was to change into black clothing, the kind typically worn by farmers. I carried my belongings and quietly tip-toed my way out of May Hall.

Standing at the entrance, I turned around and took one final look at May Hall. Perhaps this might be the last time I'll see this beautiful hostel and my friends. In the silence of my heart, I quietly bade them farewell, closed the door behind me, and sneaked out to the rendezvous point outside the Peninsula Hotel in Kowloon.

* * *

Since the day the Japanese invaded Hong Kong, we had only one thing in mind: escape. But we could not flee southwards as the Japanese had occupied much of Southeast Asia. The only place of safe refuge was Free China, that is, the remaining territories under General Chiang Kai-shek that had not fallen to the Japanese.

Despite being occupied by the Japanese, the British Government in London still regarded Hong Kong as its colony. Owing to its sense of responsibility to look after the people of Hong Kong, the British set up the British Relief Council in Guangdong province, south of mainland China. This was the nearest safe point from which the British could help refugees from their "colony."

Two professors from Hong Kong University (HKU) successfully fled Hong Kong for Free China in February 1942. They were Professor Gordon King and Professor Linsay Ride. Professor King managed to gain the support of the Chinese Government and the British authorities to set up the HKU Relief Council. And together with Professor Ride, they carefully coordinated escape plans to help HKU students find safe passage into Free China. Once the students arrived in China, the HKU Relief Council would help make arrangements for them to resume their studies.

To facilitate the escape, the HKU Relief Council despatched agents back to HKU. If we wanted to flee the Japanese, they had an escape plan prepared for us. It was a message of hope, and one that spread discreetly through word of mouth from student to student.

Eventually, I was connected with an agent. Trusting him was a great act of faith. There was no way to determine if he was actually working for the HKU Relief Council or if he was working for the Japanese trying to root out would-be escapees. I hated the uncertainty. I hated the fear that one fine day, he might just betray us all. But I had no better options available. I either had to risk my life and trust him to liberate me, or give up and continue living each day under the harsh conditions of the Japanese occupation.

The agents arranged the escapes in batches and at varying intervals so as not to arouse the suspicions of the Japanese. Each batch was limited to no more than ten people, as smaller groups were less conspicuous. For security reasons, the agents kept their identities secret. We only met them twice, but even then, they wore masks to hide their identities. On our first meeting, they briefed us on what to take on the trip and what to expect along the way. Our second meeting took place just before the day of our departure, where the agents told us where to go and who to meet.

These agents were like phantoms. They were non-existent outside of these two meets, but I was quite certain that these agents were watching us from a distance to ensure that none of us could compromise the mission in any way.

After the first meeting, I kept myself busy preparing for the arduous journey. The preparation was not easy. We had to buy numerous supplies. But this was a problem for many of us as the war had stopped all regular remittances sent by our families, and our money was frozen in the banks. We also had to buy some items of value that we could easily carry them on the journey. We were told that these valuable items would come in handy in the event that our funds dried out. We could sell or barter them along the journey, when necessary.

While many of us were preparing our supplies for the escape, a young Burmese boy of ethnic Chinese origin approached us. He was too young to be a university student. Nonetheless, he brought us news that his relative, Aw Boon Haw, wanted to meet the students of HKU. Aw Boon Haw and his brother, Aw Boon Par, were famous throughout Asia for their family's medicinal balm that could alleviate all kinds of aches and pains. It was known as Tiger Balm and the Aw brothers had amassed a fortune manufacturing and selling it.

We were all very excited that Aw Boon Haw wanted to meet us. And I was quite lucky to be in the delegation that went to meet him in his grand villa at Causeway Bay, where he graciously offered us tea.

Over tea, he told us, "You young people have the right idea in going to China. I would like all of you to have the opportunity to go to China because that is where the future is. For those of you who want to go, I would like to offer you some financial assistance. I wish you all the best of luck."

With that, he gave each of us a HKD$500 loan, and told us that we can repay him when we are able to do so. He called it a "loan" in order to save our pride, but it was clearly a gift, as he did not require us to sign any documents. After which, he directed his staff to provide us whatever medical items we needed from his store.

We left Causeway Bay that evening overwhelmed with gratitude and joy at the generosity of the man. We were greatly relieved as we now had the much needed funds to prepare for our journey.

I was among the last batch of students to leave Hong Kong. While awaiting my turn, I cultivated very good friendships with the other HKU students, who like me, were eagerly waiting for our appointed date of escape. The generous funds provided by Aw Boon Haw made it easy for us to acquire our supplies. In no time, we were ready to depart at a moment's notice. All we had to do was wait, as the date, time and place of escape were not revealed to us until the second meeting.

While waiting for our day of departure, we gathered in May Hall each day to pour out our frustrations and our anxieties, our hopes and our fears upon one another — even though we were relatively strangers. We needed each other's company as the uncertainty filled us with an immense sense of dread.

Finally, after days of anticipation, we had our second meeting, and we were instructed to meet at the rendezvous point in the wee hours of the morning. From there we will make our departure.

***

5 August 1942

Peninsula Hotel, Kowloon

The rendezvous point was behind the Peninsula Hotel. I counted the people around me. There were 25 people altogether, two of whom were our guides. Our guides were Lau Teng Kee and Chiang Lee Hai. Lau was from Malaya, and he had completed his third year of medical studies when the Japanese invaded. Chiang was an arts student who grew up in Hong Kong, and he was also the agent who had briefed us in the previous two meets.

The rest were students dressed in a similar manner like me. We had been instructed to disguise ourselves as common folk as the sight of students in lorries would arouse much suspicion. There were women in our midst, but it was hard to discern who's who in the shadows. The women had cut their hair short into a crew cut, and they had to wrap their chests tightly so as to look like men.

Ours was the largest group to escape Hong Kong, and it was quite unusual as the earlier batches were limited to at most ten people. I could sense that many of us were worried about the numbers. But we did not question our guides. We had to trust them.

The atmosphere was incredibly tense. There was hope, yet a lot of anxiety and fear. What if we got caught? We had heard of a fellow student who was caught by the Japanese and killed out in the open, in full view of everyone on the streets. He was not given a chance to explain himself. There was no trial, only a swift execution with a bullet through the head. This was the fate that awaited us if the Japanese caught us trying to escape.

There were two freight trucks parked on the side of the road. These trucks were en route to a Japanese military base in Fan Ling (up north in the New Territories of Hong Kong), as part of their regular delivery schedule, and so it would not arouse much suspicion.

The guides instructed us to put our books and other necessities at the bottom of the cargo holding area of the truck, and to sit on top of our books. Academic books are a giveaway sign that we were students. This was the least we could do to hide our identities as students from the Japanese, if they were ever to conduct an inspection.

Once we were all aboard the trucks, the drivers started the engines. And thus began our journey out of Hong Kong.

* * *

There were many checkpoints from Kowloon all the way to Fan Ling. At each checkpoint, Japanese guards were supposed to inspect, or at least 'look into' the trucks before letting them pass. We had to find opportune moments to get through these checkpoints, such as in the early hours of the morning when the guards were tired and sleepy.

Each time the truck stopped at a checkpoint, we held our breaths, out of fear that a Japanese guard would discover us hiding inside. It was intensely stressful.

In order to make the guards more at ease, our resourceful drivers plied them with strong *sake* (a Japanese liquor), taking the time to chat and drink with them. The drivers were well-trained agents. And given the numerous trips they have done, they had become quite skilled at playing games with the guards.

Fortunately, every guard we encountered indulged in the *sake*, and duly waved the trucks through without checking. We passed through every checkpoint undisturbed.

Eventually, we arrived at Fan Ling. There, we disembarked and walked a long distance towards the jetty at Sha Tau Kok (which means Sand Head Point), northeast of the New Territories. As we were in close proximity to a Japanese military base, there was a high chance of getting caught and slaughtered. We had to move fast and as stealthily as possible.

We arrived at Sha Tau Kok at around 5 o'clock in the evening. It was a small but sleepy fishing village. On the other side of the ocean was Guangdong, a part of Free China. Here was a glimpse of the freedom that awaited us. And for a brief moment, we felt a sense of liberation and joy. But all that quickly fell apart when one of the villagers informed our guides that the Japanese had wind of our presence in the area. They were coming for us.

Some young boys from the village had spotted us from a distance while we were walking, and they informed the Japanese about us. These kids had been recruited as informers for the enemy, but they were too young to understand what was going on, or the significance of their actions.

According to the villager, those boys had also informed the Japanese about the presence of many young women in our group. We were very troubled by this news. From the stories of the atrocities committed since the occupation, we knew for certain that the soldiers weren't just coming for us, they were hungry for our women.

It was not possible for us to sail away to safety. The boat was only scheduled to arrive at the jetty much later, in the early hours of the morning. Our guides began planning for a contingency. One of them found a small house far away from the jetty. We gathered the young women and hid them in a room inside that house together with all our possessions.

The rest of us men were scattered all over the village. We acted as if we were busily preoccupied with some kind of work, as if we were a part of the community. On top of that, the guides sent some of us, myself included, onto a boat. There, we had to pretend that we were fishermen going about our usual routine.

The sun had almost set, and true enough, the Japanese troops arrived, their rifles mounted with bayonets. They looked like they were ready for a fight. You could see the fury burning in their eyes. They spotted us on the boat and marched towards us, wearing the most ferocious facial expression I had ever seen. They boarded our boat, and stared straight into our eyes, with bayonets pointed in our faces. We were absolutely terrified. I could feel the sweat profusely rolling down the back of my head. The few of us on the boat managed to muster up the courage to feign ignorance, and denied the company of women in our midst. To prove the point, we invited them to search the boat.

The soldiers did not trust our claims, and began searching the boat. In the end, they found nothing. In an act of spite and petty disgust, they seized whatever belongings we had on the boat and set them ablaze in a bonfire right in front of us. They then hurled threats at us before finally storming off.

We were incredibly fortunate. No one got hurt. But the incident left us all shaken and utterly terrified.

After the incident, we knew we needed a change in plans. It was no longer safe for us to wait for the boat to arrive at Sha Tau Kok. The Japanese soldiers may return again, and there would be no second chance. We would be like sitting ducks, highly vulnerable at any moment.

The contingency plan was to abandon the boat, and walk over to "no-man's land" on foot. This was a strip of land that was neither under the control of the Japanese, nor was it under the control of Chinese nationalist forces. It was a lawless land ruled by bandits. We regrouped and immediately made haste toward "no-man's land." In that moment of haste, we neglected stealth and were spotted by Japanese troops from a distance. They shouted curses at us and began pursuing us.

The moment we heard their shouts, we began running for our lives. Fear and terror filled our hearts and minds. The only thought that raced through my head was: don't look back, just keep running.

After what felt like an eternity, we finally made it, all 25 of us. It was unbelievable! We made it into "no-man's land." We could no longer hear the shouts of our pursuers. The soldiers had given up chase. We had succeeded in fleeing from the Japanese.

But that was not the end of our troubles. Now that we were in the lawless land of bandits, there was nothing but uncertainty. Would the bandits consider us friends or foe? Would they harm us or help us?

Eventually, we encountered a group of bandits. They were armed with weapons and demanded that we paid for our "protection." That is, they would do us no harm as long as we gave them money. And so we did, reluctantly. We paid them, and they left us unharmed as we travelled through their territory till we eventually reached a jetty. There, we boarded a boat and headed towards Free China.

Hours later, we finally made landfall. But we had no idea where we were. It looked like we had arrived in the middle of nowhere. Were we safe or still in danger? There was absolutely no way of telling. We had no choice but to walk further in land to find out.

* * *

7 August 1942

Danshui, Guangdong Province, Free China

Walking for a day and a half, we arrived at a small village, called Danshui, situated on the south-east of Guangdong province. It was already evening, and the sun was beginning to set. At the distance, we noticed a flag fluttering on a hill. On closer inspection, it was the Chinese Nationalist flag flying majestically before the sun. It was, for me, one of the most beautiful and welcoming sight to behold.

At the sight of the flag, I was immediately overwhelmed with strong feelings of relief, pride, and joy. At long last, I was free from the fear and anxiety that plagued me throughout the Japanese occupation in Hong Kong. And for the first time in my life, I had set foot on the land of my ancestors, the land I had long been taught in my childhood days as my motherland.

I paused for a moment, and in that silence, offered a prayer of thanks to God.

Danshui was not our intended destination, but at least we were safe. We began openly discussing our travel plans with the villagers, and made preparations for the next part of our trip.

The discovery of this village also gave us a chance to rest. We found a small hotel and stayed a night there. A restful sleep to conclude two harrowing days of escape.

* * *

After a well-deserved night's rest, we left Danshui and began making our way to Kukong (present day Shaoguan), the war-time capital of Guangdong province. Even though much of Guangdong had been occupied by the Imperial Japanese Army, there were still some pockets of towns and routes protected by Chiang Kai-shek's army. So it was by these secure paths that we travelled.

By this stage of the journey, we all looked very unkempt. Our clothes were tattered and shabby. There was never a proper supply of water, and we had to carefully ration out whatever we had brought with us. We were acutely aware of the hazards of falling ill, and so we had to be extremely careful not to consume suspect water or unhygienic food. We could not afford to come down with food poisoning or any other illness that would render us unfit to complete our journey.

After more than a day of walking, we finally arrived at the village of Huizhou, another small town on a river bank downstream of the East River. There was a small riverboat manned by a crew of about ten members. We waited by the riverbank while our guides handled the negotiations. From afar, we could see our guides bargaining intensely to get a reasonable price.

As soon as the deal was struck, our guides waved at us to come over. We boarded the boat and began journeying upstream for about seven days. The 25 of us occupied the central section of the boat, while the boat's crew occupied the bow (front) and stern (rear). The boat was very old and equipped with a small outboard motor, which was unable to produce enough power to drive the boat upstream in the strong currents.

When the river was deep enough, the crew would row the boat. It didn't help that we were going upstream with so many of us on board. Some of the crew members stood at the back and used very thick and strong bamboo poles to push the boat forward. This required an immense amount of effort. The entire time, we witnessed them groaning with each push, their bodies dripping with sweat. When we encountered sand bars and shallow stretches, the crew would haul thick ropes across their bodies, jumped overboard onto the riverbank, and together, they dragged the boat inch by inch over the obstacles. At times, they had to go down on all fours to push, pull, shove and haul the boat along. We assisted by getting off the boat, and walked along the riverbank to lighten the load. We were happy to do this as it gave us opportunities to stretch our legs and gain some respite from the cramped conditions on board. For want of exercise, some of our boys joined the crew in hauling the boat.

One of the biggest incentives we had to disembark was when our boat passed by fruit farms along the river. We got off the boat so that we could pick fresh fruits, such as longans and lychees. The farmers were happy to share their fruits with us as they could see that we were student refugees fleeing the war. These fruits were as much a treat as they were a necessity for us to supplement our diet and to keep us healthy.

Whenever our boat arrived at a village, we made a stopover and the female members of the crew would go ashore to buy provisions. They prepared two meals for us each day, and we enjoyed fresh fish, meat and vegetables. We were reasonably well fed on the boat.

While we did spot Japanese planes flying over us on the first two days, the rest of the days passed smoothly without any incident. Overall, the boat ride was pleasant and quite relaxing. This was the first time in our escape that we could relax a little. We passed the time sharing our life stories and sang songs. One of the students, Charlie Lim, had brought his guitar with him. He'd strum his guitar in the evenings after dinner, and we'd have a sing-a-long session.

* * *

14 August 1942

Loulong, Guangdong Province, Free China

After seven memorable days on the river, we finally arrived at Loulong. Our guide told us that we had made history as there had never been such a large group of student refugees on a single trip.

There were 23 of us students in total, and we had successfully made it. After all that hardship we had endured, we got along very well with each other, and bonded together because of our common plight.

It was sad that this was the moment when we had to go our separate ways. Some of us intended to push a little farther to Kukong, others had plans elsewhere. There were no buses, and so we had to rely on trucks that passed through. It was incredibly difficult to say goodbye to one other, but with heavy hearts, we did.

Our guides helped us to flag passing trucks for their assistance. Each truck could only carry two passengers at a time. And so our group shrunk in numbers, two at a time, as we bid them farewell, not knowing if we would ever cross paths again.

Chapter 5

STRUGGLE

It took me some time before I found a driver who was willing to take me and one of my companions to Kukong. My companion got a sit at the front with the driver. I, on the other hand, was given a "seat" that was actually a small space in between a pile of goods at the back of the truck. The rear door was locked from the outside, and I was morbidly aware that if the truck overturned in an accident, I would not be able to make an exit.

The ride was highly dangerous, stressful, and uncomfortable. The truck travelled along gravel roads with large potholes and narrow paths winding along mountain ridges. We were almost suffocated by dust all the way, and I found myself tearing constantly from the incessant irritation.

I started counting the days that had passed. It had been about nine months since the Japanese invaded Hong Kong. Nine months of the grueling hardships of war. I can only thank my father. I had seen my father struggle throughout his life for the sake of our family, and he deeply inculcated in me the value of endurance. If not for him, I doubt I would have been able to endure this much hardship till now.

* * *

My father, Ho Kok Lim, was born in China in a small provincial town in Guangdong province called Shunde. He left China in 1902, and set sail for Malaya in the hopes of finding fortune abroad. However, the first few years in Malaya was a life of bitter hardship.

As a Chinese migrant worker in a British colony, he was subjected to many humiliating experiences. One encounter etched deeply in his memory was when he and many other fellow Chinese immigrants were — for the sake of a medical check-up — forced to strip naked in a group and were herded around like cattle on their way to the abattoir.

Nevertheless, despite the numerous hardships, he managed to successfully establish himself in the shoe trade. He opened his own shop in Ipoh, and called it, Heng Woh (meaning "prosperity and well-being" or "harmony and peace"). My father was ingenious and entrepreneurial. While other shoemakers in Ipoh made shoes by simply gluing together the various parts they had, my father went beyond such simple techniques. He endeavoured to perfect his craft in creating high-quality shoes, and his work stood out in the land. Both the locals and the expatriates recognised the quality of his workmanship, and his reputation and fame soared throughout Ipoh as a craftsman of high-quality shoes. The business was booming for him. And it was because of this that he was able to earn enough to raise ten children and give us the best education he could afford.

Despite his limited education, he was well-versed in the teachings and practices of the Confucian tradition. Confucianism was his guiding philosophy through life, and it shaped his person and his behaviour. He was a firm believer of teaching by example, and by his manner of conduct, he was able to profoundly impart to us the Confucian values of filial piety, loyalty, family unity, diligence, and most of all, the importance of education. These values were more than just moral concepts or ideals discussed in the abstract. They were lived out each and every single day through the daily interactions we had together as a family. He loved to discuss his philosophy passionately with us, and we could see that he was a man who abided by every precept he taught.

Of all the values my father imparted to us, the one precept that stood out and kept me going since I left Ipoh, was *"ngaai"* (捱 in Mandarin, *ai*). My father used to teach me that to *ngaai* is to endure, to struggle, to put up with the difficulties that lay ahead even if we could not see an end to the hardship. No matter how tough life can be, you must keep up with it. Accept the hardship, persevere, and go through it all.

My father didn't just teach this to me in words, he lived his entire life around the precept. From my earliest memories as a child, I had been witnessing my father *ngaai* through it all. It was very clear to our family that he struggled to raise all ten of his children. He also felt a deep responsibility to his workers whom he treated as part of his family. The responsibilities he shouldered were great, and he took great pains to fulfil his duty as father, husband, and boss, devoting all his attention and energy to his shoe business, just so that he could afford to raise us well.

Each day, he manned the shop from morning till late in the evening. He went out of his way to visit his European customers far out in the plantation areas and rendered the utmost of his craftsmanship, so as to win them over as his principal clients. And yet, despite the success of his business, never once did he indulge in personal comforts and pleasures. No, he sacrificed all of them for the welfare of his family, and his extended family of Heng Woh.

My father was a living testament of what it meant to *ngaai* for a greater cause. Hardship can make us myopic to only see the present difficulties and forget the big picture. He demonstrated to me how the immediate gains of giving up were miniscule compared to the greater gains one could acquire for others just by enduring through the struggle, no matter how long it may last, even if it goes on for years.

I know this for a fact because I gained so much from my father's *ngaai*. If not for him, I would not have been able to enjoy the education, privileges and opportunities that I had experienced throughout my life. I am the fruit of his labour, the fruit of his ngaai.

How much more can others gain if I too followed the example of my father and *ngaai* for their sake?

* * *

16 August 1942

Kukong, Guangdong Province, Free China

After two long and painful days, we finally arrived in Kukong. This war-time capital town was significant in many ways. This was where the British Relief Council, the Hong Kong University (HKU) Relief Council, and many other relief centres were located. The town was filled with refugees from various parts of war-torn China. It was a tragic sight to behold.

Nonetheless, I felt a sense of relief to see some familiar faces once again. A few of my companions from our recent escape had chosen to come here too. We met up and traded stories of our discomforting road trip. It seemed that we all had encountered the same treacherous experience, but thankfully, none of us met with any mishap.

We reached out to the HKU Relief Council to assist us in continuing our studies. Students coming from Hong Kong were mainly sent to the Sun Yat-sen (Zhongshan) University. However, for those who could afford it, most students chose to study in Chongqing, the capital of Free China at that time, where the best universities were located. Moreover, Chongqing was a city in the West, far away from the advancing Japanese army.

After some time of waiting, I was, as expected, allocated a place in the Sun Yat-sen University. Unfortunately, because of the war, the university was relocated to the small village of Pingshi. Much as I had wanted to study in Chongqing, I was strapped for cash, and so was obliged to travel to Pingshi instead.

The war changed our priorities. Staying alive was paramount. What we chosed and where we studied ceased to be a major priority. We were quite content to be given the opportunity to resume our studies. I was extremely grateful to HKU for their assistance.

Nonetheless, I knew that life as a student refugee, especially in a small village with little means to spare would be incredibly tough. As I made my way to Pingshi, I made a firm resolution to do my best to settle down and focus on my studies.

* * *

Pingshi, Guangdong Province, Free China

Pingshi was a nondescript collection of traditional dwellings and country people situated in the north of Guangdong. There were many houses and shops connected to a main road, and these buildings were built very closely together. Not too far away from the village centre, was a small hill where the Sun Yat-Sen University was located.

Everything at the Sun Yat-Sen University was makeshift. It had relocated its campus more than once due to the Japanese invasion. The campus was spread over the hill. Many of the classrooms were once residential houses. The rooms within those houses had been converted into classrooms for our lectures. The facilities were sparse as the university kept losing books and equipment each time they relocated. Some small houses were converted into offices to handle student enrolments and administration. The lecturers were part-timers who offered their services to educate us. And even they did not have their own offices. Instead, they were spared some rooms with which they could use for discussions.

There were no proper buildings to house students, so we had no choice but to source for our own accommodation. Thankfully, I found a room in a student hostel operated by the Chinese Christian missionaries, Pastor John Yong and his wife. They ran a hostel service to look after student refugees like myself. I was fortunate to receive a private room. It was a very simple setup. All the room had was a bed, a table, and a chair. Nonetheless, the location of the hostel was great, as it was quite conveniently situated within walking distance of the campus. More importantly, I enjoyed the company of my host. Pastor Yong came from Borneo, and the fact that we shared a common language and background led to a friendship that made me feel at home in a land that was so foreign to me.

Unfortunately, I had a tough time getting a good night's sleep while I was at Pingshi. As soon as night fell, and the hustle and bustle of human activity faded away, I was left with an eerie feeling that I could never shake off. It did not help that the roads were paved with pebbles. That merely amplified the sound of footsteps. No matter what hour of the night it was, I could always hear somebody walking near me. It was not a pleasant feeling to have as I lay alone on my bed. To make matters worse, every night without fail at three-hour intervals, the village time-keeper would make his rounds around the village to announce the time. He did this by striking a wooden box-like contraption that interrupted my sleep and forced me to contend with the eeriness of the night.

What I paid for in rent only covered lodging. Meals were not included, and I had very limited funds left. It took me a while to finally figure out a frugal diet that worked for me. Fortunately, some ingredients were really affordable as they were abundant in season. For about ten to twenty cents each day, I could sustain myself on tangerines, a bag of soya beans, eggs and rice. Each morning, I would drink soy milk and eat five tangerines. These were rich in protein and vitamins. If at any point I felt hungry, I would snack on soya beans and some tangerines. I looked forward to the evenings as that would be the time when I treated myself to a meal comprising a large bowl of steamed rice and an egg, drizzled over with soy sauce for taste. On some days, I was lucky to have the addition of vegetables or a salted egg.

Life in Pingshi was tough. It was an ever-constant struggle, and a reminder to *ngaai* as my father did. Each day, I had to maintain a high level of discipline to maintain such a regimen so as not to deplete what little funds I had remaining. Every day, I struggled to focus on my studies. It was difficult given the limited resources, the lack of a proper study environment, and the ever constant presence of hunger. This was the same for the other student refugees. Life was tough.

It certainly did not help that a dark shadow was constantly looming over our sojourn in Pingshi. The Japanese forces were not too far from us, and it was only a matter of time before they come to this small village. The anxiety of having to face an attack on this village was constantly on the back of our minds.

Under such trying circumstances, it was very difficult for us student refugees to persist in our studies. Some gave up their studies to find work as they could not cope with their financial difficulties.

I did my very best to adapt and to endure the struggles that life in Pingshi presented, but it did not help that my funds were running dry as the days went by. I needed to find part-time work to support myself. Each day, I would pick up the newspapers in the hope of finding an advertisement for a part-time job. I was not too optimistic about it. Jobs were hard to come by as the war had ruined the economy. I had no intention of dropping out from my studies. But struggling through the difficulties each day felt like a personal battle with myself. After a month, I started growing weary from having to struggle on a daily basis. My morale dipped, and I felt like I was at the lowest point in my life.

One day, I chanced upon an advertisement in the local newspaper, inviting young men to join the Chinese Air Force (CAF) as cadet pilots. I was transfixed by this idea. I had never considered this option, but the possibility of becoming a pilot and fighting against the Japanese forces in China really appealed to me. The people in my formative years had imbued in me a strong sense of Chinese nationalism. I had always wanted a chance to contribute in some way towards the betterment of China. Applying for the Air Force was an opportunity to express my patriotism and my love for the motherland, and to lay down my life, if necessary.

Realistically, I knew I had a very low chance of being accepted. I had a small stature and lacked the required qualifications. But given the conditions in Pingshi, what more had I to lose?

I submitted the application.

Chapter 6

THE DOOR OF DESTINY

Guilin, Guangxi Province, Free China

Several days later, I received a phone call. It was the China Air Force (CAF) Recruitment Centre. To my great surprise (and to the surprise of my friends), the CAF invited me to attend an interview and medical examination at their Recruitment Centre in Guilin. Guilin was an important airbase, specially set up by the United States Fourteenth Air Force to support Chinese operations against the Japanese. I could not afford the trip to Guilin, but fortunately the CAF sent me a train ticket and a small allowance for the journey.

When I arrived at Guilin, I learnt that it was also another designated student relief centres, with large numbers of student refugees from Hong Kong, Macau, and Guangzhou. Among them were a number of Malayan Chinese students. I befriended many of them, and they in turn helped me to find accommodation. Interestingly, I chose the strangest place to stay. It was on board a boat on the Lijiang River. It was affordable, quiet, and most of all, clean. In fact, the waters were so clean and clear that you could see the bottom of the river, and I enjoyed a dip with the fishes each day.

Over the next couple of days, I spent most of my time in a small restaurant, gathered with many other aspiring pilots. We were all waiting our turn for the written and medical examinations. As the days went by, I watched as many of them returned from the Recruitment Centre with their faces downcast. They had failed the examinations. Most of them lacked the necessary academic requirements in the first place. But fortunately for them, they were given the opportunity to become co-pilots, navigators, or radio operators for the Chinese National Aviation Corporation (CNAC), which was the only commercial airline at that time. At the very least, these young men were given a chance to fulfil their dreams of becoming pilots, not in combat roles, but in transporting essential war materiel.

Eventually, the time came for my examination. For the written examination, I had to sit for three written papers. The first was on Chinese History and Political Philosophy. Luck was on my side that day. The paper was on Dr. Sun Yat-sen's political philosophy on the topic of the "Three Principles of the People," which I had studied in depth during my term at Hong Kong's Lingnan University. That was a breeze for me. The second paper was on General Aviation, Science, and Mathematics, and the third paper was on English and General Knowledge. I was very fortunate to have studied these topics previously in Ipoh and in Hong Kong University (HKU).

I could not help but feel that Providence had directed me by ordering events along my path in life. Had my father not sent me to a Christian mission school in my formative years, I would not have been able to do well for the English and General Knowledge Paper. Had I not enrolled into Lingnan University, I would not have been able to pass the paper on Sun Yat-sen's philosophy. Had I not enrolled in the sciences during my first year at HKU, I would not have been able to pass the paper on General Aviation, Science, and Mathematics. Had I not been in Pingshi, I would not have seen the advertisement calling for recruits for the CAF. It was as if God's invisible hand had been moving me to overcome one obstacle after another in preparation for my destiny as a pilot.

However, that great optimism in fulfilling my destiny as a pilot slowly fizzled when I failed the visual acuity test during the medical examination. I was unable to read the bottom line of the eye chart. I was extremely disappointed that day, and returned to the same restaurant to drown my sorrow with my newfound friends.

It was there that I met Yau Sow Wah, a fellow Malayan from my hometown of Ipoh. He was very keen to join the CAF, but he lacked the matriculation certificate. Since we were both from Ipoh, he was determined that at least one of us should get into the CAF. I lamented about my failure in the visual acuity test, and complained that the lighting in the room was a little dim to properly read the bottom line of the test chart. Had the room been a little brighter, I would have managed to read the entire chart and passed the test.

Hearing this, Yau assured me that he would try to help me. He left the restaurant and found the examiner who tested my eyesight. I don't know how he did it, but Yau managed to persuade the examiner to let me re-take the test under improved lighting. The next day, I was given that second chance, and I passed the test. I was overjoyed! I was on my way to becoming a pilot.

All it took was Yau's simple request to unlock the door to my destiny in aviation.

Chapter 7

A NEW LIFE

4 January 1943

China Air Force Recruitment Centre, Guilin, Guangxi Province

Today's the day where I would set off on a long journey to realise my destiny as a pilot. The thought of becoming a pilot was still so surreal in my mind. I was so enthralled by the very thought of it that I could not bear lying on my bed any longer. I got up very early in the morning, got dressed, and made my way to the China Air Force Recruitment Centre. We were instructed to report there early in the morning, where we would be transported to our first place of training.

Upon arriving at the Recruitment Centre, I was pleasantly surprised to see another 24 cadets waiting around the area. It turned out that I wasn't the only one too eager to begin our journey as pilots. Some of the cadets shared stories of their aspirations to fly, some shared their imaginations of how they would defeat the enemy when they become full-fledged pilots. Their stories made waiting a lot more tolerable, and they fuelled our own imaginations about what was to come. We were all roused up with great excitement.

At the appointed time, an officer of the Recruitment Centre came out to greet us. He instructed us to board a nearby military truck.

From the outside, the truck seemed rather small, but there was just enough space to barely squeeze all 25 of us. We boarded the truck, and once we were all crammed in, the officer wished us the best of luck and bid us farewell.

The driver started the engine, and thus began our journey.

* * *

We were transported first to Yibin, along the treacherously dangerous Guilin-Yibin road, notoriously known as "the road of a hundred bends." Along the way, we came across many student refugees fleeing from various parts of war-torn China. They were making their way up to Chongqing. Whenever a truck pulled over, big groups of student refugees would rush over, begging for a lift to get a little closer to Chongqing. They were desperate as it was already winter, and they urgently needed to complete their journey, or at least find a more permanent resting stop to shelter from the freezing cold. I felt great sympathy for them. But unfortunately, there was nothing I could do as our truck was already packed like sardines to the brim.

We arrived at the barracks in Yibin where we were supposed to carry out our first phase of training. Unfortunately, the enemy had subjected the entire area to incessant raids and cut off our supply lines. There were insufficient provisions to sustain us, and limited fuel remaining to carry out any flight training.

And so, before we could even settle down in Yibin, we were promptly told to pack our bags and board the truck. We had been ordered to travel farther down south to Kunming in Yunnan province.

* * *

China Air Force Flight School, Kunming, Yunnan Province

After a couple of days on a long and bumpy road, we finally arrived in Kunming. Kunming is famously known as the "City of Spring" for its year-long temperate climate. It was situated on a plateau and protected by mountains on three sides, with the massive Lake Dian to the south. Here, we joined the 16th class of the Chinese Air Force Academy. Altogether there were 120 of us cadets comprising students and military graduates hailing from all over China, with a significant portion of overseas Chinese originating from various parts of Southeast Asia, such as Malaya and Singapore.

Once at Kunming, they wasted no time to commence our pre-flight training. The training was a long and arduous process. One aspect of it was classes on the basic principles of flying, meteorology, and air navigation. Learning was a breeze for me, and I enjoyed these classes, especially since they were most relevant to my future as a pilot. And, as we had to complete our training in the United States of America, there was a mandatory course in English, which I naturally excelled since I grew up learning and speaking the language.

However, one aspect of pre-flight training that I strongly resented was the arduous basic military training and physical fitness routines, which were intended to toughen us up. Each day, as soon as reveille sounded, we had to complete a set of routine tasks with precision. Daily chores had to be completed meticulously and in the prescribed manner. For example, when making your bed, the sheets had to look as smooth as freshly cut *tofu* (beancurd). I was not very good in this respect, so I was punished for it repeatedly.

I was desperate, and began seeking help from my fellow course mates. Eventually, I became friends with Kasun Chu Pee, a Tibetan who graduated from the Chinese Military Academy in early 1942. He was eager to learn English from me, and in exchange, he agreed to help me make my bed according to the regimental requirements. We struck a deal, and we became very good friends as time went on. Henceforth, I was not called out for failing to do my chores properly ever again.

Every activity during the course of our training was strictly governed by the clock, including the most basic of human activities. If you did not complete your breakfast by a designated time, you had to forego the remaining portion. And contrary to the principles of good health, we had our routine runs and other exhausting physical exercises immediately after breakfast. The intent was to toughen us so that we were fit for combat. Those cadets trained in the Army Academy breezed smoothly through the regimental way of life. But for college students like myself, it was a great challenge. I struggled immensely to adjust to the regimental training.

At this phase of training, the attrition rate among cadets was very low. The few who dropped out were physically unfit and could not cope with strict military routine. This gruelling phase of training was tough! It was the sheer determination for me to press on. I kept reminding myself that there was no other option for me than to succeed. My journey to becoming a pilot was my one-way ticket for survival. I had already dropped out of university. There was no chance for re-admission. And dropping out from the China Air Force meant having to join the millions of refugees struggling to survive in the tough cold winter in China. There's no turning back now. I just have to struggle through it all and endure the hardships. It was what my father taught me, and what he did through life to raise me.

* * *

As the Japanese advanced farther into China, there was a change to our training itinerary. After we completed our pre-flight training, we had to travel to India for primary flight training, and later to the United States of America to complete the rest of our training as pilots. We had to ensure that our passports were valid for travel to those countries.

At that time, I was ignorant of foreign relations and diplomatic matters. I did not think that I would have any issues. After all, I was able to travel from Malaya to Hong Kong. My officers helped me to check the validity of my passport. Unlike the other British colonies, Ipoh was part of the Federated Malay States (FMS) under the protection of the British empire. Though I held a British passport, I had no citizenship status at all. Instead, stamped on my passport were the words, "British Protected Person of the Federated Malay States." As a protected person, I had several travel restrictions, many countries that I had completely no access to at all. I had no idea about this!

I had a rude shock learning that I was a second-class citizen, an inferior "protected" being barred from travelling around the world through no fault of my own simply because of the contingent fact that I happened to be born in Ipoh at a time when the British were the colonial masters of the land.

I was visibly upset and anxious that I would not be able to complete my training. But my officers assured me that everything will be alright.

Several days later, my officers approached me. True to their word, they issued me a new passport bearing the words, "The Republic of China," on the front cover. They were very understanding of my situation and quietly applied to the authorities for me to have a Chinese passport.

The passport was handed to me in an unceremonious manner. Yet, the moment I received it in my hands, it was a moment of great pride and joy for me. I opened the passport and next to my name was the status saying that I was a citizen of China, and a member of the Kuomintang (KMT, the ruling party of China). My status was upgraded. I was not a "protected" person anymore. I wasn't just given a new lease of life by joining the Air Force, I was given a new life as a citizen, a part of something bigger. I was filled with a great sense of pride and patriotism to be officially acknowledged as a member, as a citizen, of the land of my ancestors.

This passport was for me, a tangible expression of my Chinese culture and heritage that my father had long imbued in me. A physical representation that this is my place of belonging. It instilled in me a greater fervour to serve the country and contribute to the war effort.

I cannot give up now. My motherland awaits my service. I am ready to lay down my life for her.

*　*　*

After months of painful struggle, I managed to pass the pre-flight training phase, and was medically cleared to move on to the next phase of the course. The primary flight training was conducted in Lahore, which was then in the northeast of India (now a part of Pakistan).

To get to Lahore, we needed to fly over the mighty Himalayas, over an area infamously known as "The Hump." It was a terribly dangerous journey, and many pilots and their crew died flying over it (over one-third of the pilots who flew over the Hump did not survive the war). Despite the dangers, this route was the only route short enough for transport aircraft to travel without refuelling. Previously, there had been a safe land route, but sections of it were cut off by Japanese forces in April 1942, so China had no choice but to use the Hump, as it was a critical route for so many operations. Chief among them was the desperate need to transport essential supplies into China to sustain the fight against the Japanese.

The terrain was hostile, and the weather unpredictable. Far away from human civilisation, pilots could not rely on airborne radio navigational aids. There were none present in the area. To fly over the Hump, pilots literally had to take their lives into their own hands as they manually negotiated a passage through the perilous mountain passes and narrow valleys. They had to be vigilant and depend on the merits of their own eyes as they cautiously steered their way through the passes of high mountains.

At that time, the only transport aircraft capable of travelling long distances across the Hump were the DC-3 Dakota and the C-46 Commando. These twin-engine propeller transport aircraft could not climb over the taller peaks. When it was necessary to make a climb, it was problematic for pilots to do so, as the aircraft was often overloaded with cargo. To make matters worse, the Hump was often fraught with density altitude problems, that prevented pilots from attempting to fly the plane higher over a mountain. When faced with a vertical obstacle in their flight path, pilots had no choice but to try to fly around it.

It did not help that the Hump was constantly plagued with thick mists and snow storms, making it difficult to fly over it. It was as good as flying blindfolded. By the time a pilot could see a mountain in the poor visibility, it was too late. Some pilots were lucky and managed to survive when bad weather unexpectedly cleared and they could make their way through the mountains visually.

But even if weather conditions were good, pilots had to deal with extremely strong winds that would unpredictably funnel through the mountains. These winds could reach 120 miles per hour (about 200 km/h), violently tossing the aircraft around like a leaf in the wind. Sometimes, pilots survived the extreme winds, but if Lady Luck was not on their side, they would have lost their bearings and be unable to navigate out of the area. There were ground aids, small radio transmitters known as Non-Directional Beacons that provided the aircraft's Automatic Direction Finders. However, these beacon signals were weak and often unreliable as they could be easily distorted by the atmospheric conditions of the terrain. Where the entire horizon was nothing but mountainous peaks with no distinctive features, it was difficult to get a sense of one's location, or where one should be heading. Many pilots and their crew met their demise as they flew around aimlessly until their aircraft ran out of fuel and crashed.

Those who survived the crash were as good as dead. Even if they could radio back to report their crash location, there was no way to reach or rescue them in the treacherous Himalayan mountains.

The journey over the Hump was a one-way ticket for many pilots. Once pilots had commenced their flight over the Hump, it was difficult or sometimes impossible to turn back as the aircraft may have insufficient fuel to return. There were also a few places in the mountainous terrain where an aircraft of that size could make a 180-degree U-turn. The spaces between mountains were too narrow for the aircraft's turning radius. Depending on the weather, the journey would take between four to six hours. It was a feat of mental endurance for the pilot to stay alert and cautious for such a long period of time. Each flight required a great deal of courage and mental stamina.

Naturally, we were quite frightful of the journey. But we were assured that we were in the good hands of an experienced pilot. As soon as the pilot received reports of good weather, we were ordered to board the plane. Favourable weather did not guarantee a safe flight, but it was the next best option to rely on. We boarded the plane and strapped ourselves tightly to our seats. The air was tense. The thought that we might crash and die out in the Himalayas filled us with much dread.

Would we make it out alive? Or would we join our fallen comrades in the Himalayas, buried within the coffin that was once the aircraft?

The plane took off. There's no turning back now.

Chapter 8

SPREADING MY WINGS

The aircraft was high up in the air, flying vertically upwards into the sky in a nose-up position. It climbed higher and higher, until the air ceased to flow across the wing surface. The engine stalled. The aircraft began falling out of the sky like a proverbial ton of bricks. It had gone into free fall. It was spiralling out of control.

I felt as if my heart was in my mouth. I was petrified. I didn't know what to do. Looking down was a bad idea. With every passing second, the buildings on the ground looked bigger and bigger. I was going to crash.

In a split-second, I suddenly remembered what I needed to do. I needed to be in control. I snapped out of my petrified state and recovered just enough calm within myself. I took a deep breath. And with that, I began executing the stall recovery action.

In a matter of seconds, I regained control of the aircraft, and landed it safely on the runway of our Flight Training Base in Lahore.

Admittedly, it was an awfully harrowing experience. Despite all that, my instructor was proud of me. I had just experienced an engine stall and succeeded in recovering the aircraft for the very first time. As cadets, we were required to perform many stalls with our instructors, and later on our own when we flew solo. This was a crucial component of our training as the engine could stall at any moment, whether it is take-off, landing, or even in mid-air. It was absolutely essential to regain control of the aircraft when a stall occurs.

* * *

April 1943

CAF Flight Training Base, Lahore, India

Divine providence was truly on our side. We had crossed the Hump safely a couple of days ago, and arrived in Ding Jian, Assam. There were some minor turbulence during the flight, but we made it out of the Hump unscathed. And after a lengthy train ride across several cities, all 120 of us cadets finally arrived safely in Lahore.

Lahore was a desert with temperatures peaking at a high of 35 degrees Celsius (95 degrees Fahrenheit). Despite the uncomfortably hot temperatures, Lahore reminded me of my home back in Ipoh, Malaya. The balmy climate, the towns, roads, fields, rubber plantations, and the way people dressed and behaved, were reminiscent of the sights, sounds, and smells that I had encountered while growing up.

The Chinese Air Force (CAF) had just taken over the Royal Lahore Flying Club and converted it into their Flight Training Base. This was necessary as other parts of China had fallen to the Japanese, and it was not safe for us to continue training there anymore. As such, we were the first cohort to undergo primary flight training in Lahore.

The main objective of this phase of training was to assess our suitability and capability for further training in the United States. We were required to clock 60 flying hours before being assessed by US Air Force officers. Those who passed were qualified to proceed to the USA for further training.

Our instructors were all Chinese nationals. They ranged from young pilots who recently completed their training with the US Air Force, to very experienced pilots who had flown for the CAF for over a decade. There were as many instructors as there were Stearman PT-17 aircraft. These were the workhorse of our training.

The instructors devised a fixed roster to ensure that we had plenty of continuous and uninterrupted flying. They also ensured the training base was well-stocked with more than enough fuel so that our training would proceed without disruptions. Fortunately for us, the weather conditions in Lahore were very favourable. There was an abundance of sunshine and clear skies, and we flew almost every day.

Our instructors needed us to learn to fly in a very short span of time. Within a period of 8–10 flying hours, we had to become competent with take-offs, keeping a constant height, flying a straight course, descending appropriately, and landing safely. Cadets who failed to master these skills within 10 hours of flying were dropped from further training and were promptly sent back to China. Approximately one in five cadets failed this initial stage of training. Some simply did not have the ability. Some did have the ability, but they could not meet the high standards demanded of them.

I felt like a baby bird learning to spread its wings. There were many moments of trepidation. But like these birds, they eventually acquire mastery over their wings and are able to soar to great heights. Similarly, despite the intense pressure to master flying in a short span of time, I was among the many cadets who succeeded in flying solo without an instructor after 5–6 hours of training.

Once we had gained the confidence to fly solo, we were schooled in advance techniques like acrobatics and formation flying. It was tough learning to master these techniques, but I absolutely loved the thrill of flying. I felt a great sense of accomplishment in mastering these manoeuvres.

* * *

Three months had passed, and we had completed our flight training. By now, each of us had clocked the necessary 60 hours of flying on the Stearman aircraft. It was time to be assessed by officers from the US Air Force.

My instructor, Captain Loo, was very confident that I would pass the assessment with flying colours. His belief in me was an important morale booster, as the entire process of testing was incredibly nerve-wrecking. There I was, performing the necessary tasks and manoeuvres up in the air, while an American officer sat behind me on the aircraft, examining my every move. There were several other American officers on the ground assessing my performance.

Not too long after I completed the assessments, I received an order to pack my bags. I was among the 80 cadets selected for further training in the USA! I was relieved and grateful for the news. All the months of hard work had paid off!

Lahore had been very good to me. Though my time here was short, I will always remember Lahore as the very place where I first learnt to spread my wings.

Chapter 9

THEY CALLED ME WINKIE

September 1943

New York

We had been sailing from Bombay to New York, via the Cape of Good Hope, on board the RMS *Queen Elizabeth*, an ocean liner operated by the Cunard Line. This was one of the many passenger liners that were converted into a troop transport ship during the war. These converted ships were admirably suited to transporting troops, as they were originally designed to carry passengers, and were fast enough to outrun German warship.

It had been an incredibly long and uneventful voyage. We spotted nothing but the sky and the sea, and the occasional rocks and islands along the way. Thankfully, we did not encounter any enemy ships along the way. It was a peaceful voyage.

"Look over there!", shouted one of my fellow cadets. He had saw something out of the ordinary.

I turned around and looked. Far across the distance was the Statue of Liberty, standing magnificently at the mouth of the Hudson River.

As the RMS *Queen Elizabeth* drew closer to New York harbour, we were confronted with the imposing size of the Statue of Liberty. It was a majestic sight to behold, and one that overwhelmed me with great emotion. We had committed our lives to fight for the liberty of our brethren back in China, and here before us stood Lady Liberty herself, as an affirmation of what we were doing.

It's been three months out at sea. And at long last, we have finally arrived safe and sound.

* * *

Williams Air Force Base, Chandler, Arizona

With no time to waste, we were quickly transported to Williams Air Force Base in Chandler, Arizona. I was amazed by the Americans and their logistical efficiency. They had well laid out barracks, administrative offices, mess halls, club rooms, sports and recreation facilities, everything proceeded according to plan, without a hitch, and with clockwork precision.

Before we could take in all the changes around us and settle down, we were required to embrace the G.I. (General Issue) way of life. We were paid a small allowance of USD$60 each. But we had no need to spend the money as everything was provided. The only time we used the money was on our off days where we would head to town for recreational activities. For accommodation, we were given a large barracks. For clothing, we were issued G.I. uniforms, which by the way, made us look very smart. For transportation, we were always ferried around on buses from one place to another for lectures or demonstrations. For food, we were issued three square meals a day, laid out in a buffet style. Meals were prepared according to the American diet, and it included a beverage and dessert.

I had no problems adjusting to the American diet. As someone coming from Ipoh, which was then administered by the British, I had been exposed to many Western dishes since young. Some of my coursemates who had never been out of China, or been exposed to anything Western in their lives, struggled greatly with the new diet. They had a hard time adapting to the new flavours and cuisines. It was a huge culture shock for them. For some, it was a big struggle that affected their morale. Yet, they did their very best to be stoic about it.

Our flight training in the US comprised five phases over one year: (1) a Pre-flight Phase at Williams Air Force Base in Chandler, Arizona; (2) a Primary Phase at Thunderbird Field in Glendale, Arizona; (3) a Basic Phase at Marana Field in Tuscon, Arizona; (4) an Advanced Phase at Douglas Field in Douglas, Arizona; and finally, (5) the Operational Training Unit (OTU) Phase at La Junta Air Force Base in Colorado.

The pre-flight training marked the start of our training under the US Air Force. Much of it was like a repeat of our training in Kunming: we had to attend aviation classes and to stay physically fit under a regimented way of life. The purpose of repeating this phase was to give us time to become acquainted with the American way of life, and to master the English language. Despite the English classes we had in Kunming, the majority of the Chinese cadets still struggled with the language. They had to attend intensive language classes here.

There were about twenty of us cadets who were from Hong Kong and Malaya, and we were capable of speaking fluent English. This made it easy for us to mingle with the other cadets on base, most of whom hailed from America, Canada, and the United Kingdom.

**

It was here that I received an "English" name. Back in Malaya, my name was written as "Ho Weng Toh," where the surname, following Chinese convention, would be at the front. However, when I came to America, I had to follow the Western convention, where the surname was written behind. On my uniform, my name was thus written as, "Weng Toh Ho." My newfound friends, ignorant of the culture behind Chinese names, mistakenly thought that "Weng" was my first name. And just as how "John" becomes "Johnny" and "Bob" becomes "Bobby," they converted "Weng" (pronounced the same way you say "Wing") into "Winkie," as a term of friendly endearment.

To be honest, I did not like the name "Winkie" at all. But I guess it was better than the nickname my Chinese friends gave me. They called me "cockroach," alluding to my small size and alacrity.

The name stuck amongst my friends in America. And from then on, they called me Winkie.

Chapter 10

FLYING SOLO

December 1943

Thunderbird Field in Glendale, Arizona

After three months of pre-flight training, we moved to Thunderbird Field in Glendale, Arizona, for our Primary Flight Training. Like the training base in Lahore, Thunderbird Field was originally a prestigious private flying club. It had everything the US Air Force needed to convert it into a flight training school. Our brief stay came complete with facilities like swimming pools, tennis courts, and a football field.

We had already clocked 60 flying hours back in Lahore on the Stearman PT-17. Here in Glendale, we were required to fly the same aircraft, and master the same tasks, such as take-off, landing, maintaining altitude, recovering from a stalled engine, just to name a few. The training was a breeze.

Towards the end of the training, we learnt that the instructors only wanted the very best pilots to progress on to the next phase of training. The flying tests they devised were demanding and difficult. While it was a great challenge for me, I managed to pass.

At the end of the day, I learnt that one-fifth of our group failed. I could see it in their eyes that they were very disappointed. Nonetheless, because they had come this far, the US Air Force gave them the opportunity to remain in Glendale, where they would be trained in related fields, such as navigators, bombardiers, and wireless operators.

For the rest of us who made it, we were soon ordered to pack. A convoy of buses came and ferried us to the Marana Air Force Base in Tuscon, Arizona.

* * *

Marana Field, Tuscon, Arizona

Marana Air Force Base stood in stark contrast from the comfortable life we enjoyed in Glendale. Calling it "spartan" would have done much injustice to the Spartans. The base was situated in the midst of a flat parched desert. There was nothing but sand. There were no signs of human life anywhere along the desert horizon. The nearest town, Tucson, was many miles away.

Here, we had to undergo Basic Flight Training, where we had to clock another 60 hours of flying. This time, it was on the Vultee BT-13 aircraft, a sophisticated aircraft that required greater technical mastery. Training spanned over a couple of months, the longest of the five training phases.

Our instructors kept us busy with tight schedules. We were up in the air, flying almost every single day, and we had to give our utmost concentration to our training. When we were not flying, we were kept busy with physical training. Eventually, the intense training took a massive toll on us emotionally and psychologically. It had been almost a year since we left China, and many of us were too tired to cope with the strong feelings of homesickness and loneliness. It was a trying period, but we did the best we could.

* * *

The weekends were our oasis in the desert, a short moment of reprieve from the arduous training and profound loneliness. Many of us travelled all the way to Tucson to visit the Chinese families that lived there. We first met them as they were part of a Chinese delegation that came to warmly welcome us on arrival to Arizona.

At first, our weekend trips were just visits to these families. But as soon as we learnt about their beautiful daughters, many of us were eager to spend our precious off days to see them. They were very friendly and extremely amiable. Over time, some of us began developing romantic relationships with these American Chinese girls.

I found myself infatuated with one such girl. Her name was Eva Lee, and she was of Mexican-Chinese descent. Her upbringing made her very different from the other Chinese girls I knew. She was friendly and very charming. I was absolutely devoted to her. I used every off day and weekend I had to religiously make a pilgrimage to Tucson just to spend time with her. As time went by, our friendship blossomed, and we shared a romantic relationship together.

But in a series of unfortunate events, our time together was abruptly interrupted.

A fellow cadet by the name of Willy Ho had disappeared and gone AWOL (Absent Without Official Leave). This incident was a major embarrassment for my commanding officer, Colonel Yang Shao

Lien, and his reputation was at stake. He discovered that I was close friends with Willy and questioned me about his whereabouts. In all honesty, I had no idea where Willy had disappeared to. But this was not an answer that satisfied Colonel Yang.

Suspecting that I was covering up for Willy, Colonel Yang made my life a living hell by restricting my movements. I could not leave the base even on my days off. I could not see Eva Lee anymore. I was devastated. I was heart-broken.

* * *

Willy Ho and I were very good friends, and our friendship started back in Guilin, China, in 1942, where I was applying to join the CAF.

Willy had the appearance of a Eurasian. He had a long nose and a fair complexion. As a child, he was adopted in Hong Kong by an English businessman and his wife. When the war broke out, his adopted father was interned by the Japanese. Willy fled to Free China and ended up in Guilin, where he earned his livelihood playing football and working as a restaurant waiter. For shelter, he spent every night sleeping on a table in the restaurant he worked.

We first met in the same restaurant where he lived and worked. That was the same restaurant where CAF aspirants gathered, waiting their turn for the examinations. Willy was inspired by the numerous CAF aspirants to become a pilot. One day, he approached me and befriended me in the hope that I could get him entry into the CAF. I was unwittingly drawn in by his charismatic personality.

I was quite amazed by Willy. Though young, he was very resourceful, and was quick to adapt to new and challenging circumstances. He was also a remarkable opportunist, and took advantage of every opening to advance himself. He used his charming personality to smooth talk his way through the CAF preliminary interviews. And he managed to get to the examination stage despite lacking the obligatory matriculation certificate!

When we sat for the written examination, he sat close to me. The CAF invigilator frequently left the room, and Willy would then lean over and copy my answers. I would not be the least surprised if he had bribed the supervisor.

We passed the examination and we journeyed every step of the way from China to Lahore, and finally to Arizona. We had become close confidantes. And I was very proud to see my close friend and fellow cadet prove himself as an excellent pilot throughout our training.

Willy stood out from all the other cadets. More than just an excellent pilot, his exuberance was in a class all of his own. When not in uniform, he dressed stylishly, with his hair neatly combed back, giving the air of a man about town. Willy knew how to have fun wherever he went, and he assimilated easily into the carefree American way of life. This proved to be his undoing as a pilot, as the attractions and opportunities for fun distracted him from the mental discipline required for the flight training programme. Perhaps it was the strenuous training that took a toll on his mind.

As his close friend, it was painful for me to observe a change in his attitude. His sense of discipline was eroding perceptibly, and he was clearly losing interest in flying. One day, Willy confided with me that if he should ever go missing, I should inform the authorities that he had left for New York to visit a relative. I had come to know Willy as a daring person, often to the point of recklessness.

This did not surprise me one bit. As a concerned friend, I cautioned him about what he was planning to do. But he was unfazed by it.

* * *

One evening, it finally happened. Willy missed a routine inspection. Our commanding officer, Colonel Yang, went about asking the cadets for information on his whereabouts. I figured New York was not a believable story, so I reported to Colonel Yang that Willy had fled to San Francisco to visit a relative. I thought San Francisco was a more plausible destination as there was a large community of Chinese living there.

Colonel Yang immediately informed the flying school authorities, and Willy was declared AWOL. Such absence was an extremely serious offence. The military police were immediately alerted to search for him in San Francisco. If arrested, he would most probably be sent back to the CAF in China, where he would be court-martialed and executed for desertion.

Willy was gone. My close friend and confidante was gone. And I could not go out to meet Eva, the love of my life. And yet our training went on uninterrupted, as if none of these had ever happened.

I had to fly solo now.

Chapter 11

FRIENDS COMING AND GOING

8 February 1944

El Paso and Southwestern Railroad Passenger Depot, Douglas, Arizona

The past couple of days have been a string of sad goodbyes to the friends I made in Tucson and Phoenix. We had completed our training at Marana, and it was time for us to move on to the next phase of training.

The saddest of all was having to bid farewell to Eva. I felt sorry for her. Just when we had started a romantic relationship, we were not allowed to spend time any time together. I was confined within the base because of Willy's sudden departure. Judging by her attitude and behaviour towards me in these past days, I guess she has no more serious thoughts about me. Perhaps she has found another love interest, or perhaps I was just imagining things. Life can be so cruel.

There's no knowing whether I'll ever get to meet Eva or any of my Tucson friends again. My fellow cadets have been telling me, "We know what is going on now, but what becomes the morrow, nobody can tell." This has certainly impacted my view of life itself. I don't know what will come tomorrow. There's so much uncertainty. The people in my life have been coming and going too quickly.

It had been a long and tiring journey.

The train comes to a stop. My fellow cadets and I arise from our seats to alight. I am surrounded by people, and yet I am alone.

All I know is that I would like to get married as soon as I return to China. At least I will have a wife by my side regardless of "what becomes the morrow." In a way, this was rather selfish of me, but with the constant coming and going of significant people in my life, what I needed now more than ever was a constant companion.

* * *

Douglas Air Field, Douglas, Arizona

Our advanced training phase was conducted in Douglas Air Field, which was just one street junction away from the border with Mexico. Douglas was a small town in a remote corner of Arizona. There wasn't much here, but it felt like heaven compared to Marana. At least civilisation was close by. As it was a very small town, there was no excitement or social life whatsoever. So we concentrated our energy and attention on our training as best as we could.

I was placed under the guidance of Lieutenant E. C. Ward, who was a very patient and kind instructor. This time, our training was on the twin-engine Cessna AT-17, a 2-seater aircraft with a retractable undercarriage. The AT-17 was capable of flying at a longer range. And this allowed us to conduct many cross-country flights to places such as Casa Grande and Tuscon in Arizona; El Paso in Texas; and Santa Ana in California. We learnt how to fly in formation, and how to fly long-distance using navigational instruments especially when flying at night. This final basic phase of flight training greatly increased my confidence as a pilot.

* * *

During my time at Douglas, I discovered what had happened to Willy, the friend who went AWOL and got me into trouble. He met a Mexican girl while he was in Phoenix, and he fell in love with her. She had convinced him to leave the CAF and stay behind in America, and Willy did just that. With funding from his half-sister (who resided in New York), Willy slipped out of the military base and crossed the border into Mexico.

Love can be such a powerful and intoxicating motivator for a young person. This was especially the case for a spirited and impulsive young man like Willy. Love compelled him to do something totally irrational like walking out on a training commitment and risk execution for desertion.

As irrational as this might have been for Willy, I completely understood what was going through his mind. Many of us, in fact, found ourselves in similar situations while in Tucson. We were tempted on so many occasions to run away, just as Willy did. The impetus was strong especially after we formed romantic relationships with the young Chinese ladies there. What kept us in line was our sense of duty and a fear of the consequences.

It was only Willy who actualised our dreams by taking the one big step that none of us dared to take. In some ways, we admired him for his foolishness and bravery.

By this stage, it wasn't just the American military police and the CAF who were looking for Willy. The Federal Bureau of Investigation (FBI) had joined the hunt. This did not stop Willy from attempting to communicate with me. Over the next couple of months, we kept in communication with each other in the form of little pieces of paper with messages scribbled onto them. These messages were then passed to me by hand through various individuals. I had no idea how he was able to accomplish this feat across many months, but I am sure he made good use of his charming personality.

By piecing the various scraps of messages together, I learnt that Willy was living a decent life in Mexico with his lover, working as a waiter and cook in a Chinese restaurant.

Willy loves challenges and often did not consider the consequences. Knowing him well, I was quite sure he would one day attempt to cross the border back to the US. I warned him repeatedly to stay away from US soil. The authorities were actively on the lookout for him. If he attempted to enter the US, Willy was sure to get caught.

*　*　*

A month had passed and we completed the first part of our training. It was at this stage that we had to choose whether to be trained as a fighter pilot or as a bomber pilot. The more daring and ambitious among us chose to be fighter pilots. The training was generally much tougher and physically more demanding. Many fighter planes had previously been shot down by the Japanese, and so the tough training was to ensure the newly minted pilots were more resilient to the stresses of war. Some added incentives of becoming a fighter pilot were the adrenalin which these daredevils craved, the adoration of 'the girls,' and higher pay. On the other hand, training to be a bomber pilot was less challenging, and the flights were less dangerous, since bomber aircraft were much heavier and less agile in the air, and were often escorted by single-engine fighters that led the way on missions.

In the end, I chose to be a bomber pilot. It seemed to me a good pathway for future employment after the war, that is, if I survived the war. I had the option to convert and become a civilian air transport pilot in the future.

This choice, however, came at a cost. The majority of my cadet friends had chosen to become fighter pilots. Their training was conducted at Luke Air Force Base in Glendale, Arizona, whereas bomber pilot training was conducted here in Douglas Air Field. Once again, it was another round of sad farewells as we parted ways.

Bomber training was conducted under the leadership of our CAF commander, Captain Lu Sheng-Jen, who was a very suave young scholar. He was one of the five CAF scholars from Beijing's prestigious universities. Captain Lu was very approachable and he shared our aspirations to complete the training as quickly as possible so that we can return and fight for China. The training spanned over a period of three months, and we flew the twin-engine Cessna AT-17 (Advanced Trainer) aircraft. By now, we were very experienced and the training went very smoothly.

***

25 March 1944

Fort Huchuca, Sierra Vista, Arizona

Occasionally, to beat the monotony of training, we would go out for excursions. I had the best time of my life on this beautiful morning. The Commanding Officer of the Post invited us, the cadets from our bomber group, out for a tour to Fort Huchuca, which was then the biggest training base for coloured people in America. We set off in three military trucks.

Along the way, we passed through Bisbee, a town situated in a deep valley. The buildings were set up in terraces, which reminded me of the good days in Hong Kong. As our trucks climbed over the Bisbee Hills, we found ourselves at the historical American town of Tombstone, which used to be one of the largest towns in the South West. True to its name, there were many tombstones in sight.

Captain Lu gave us a fascinating brief of the town's history. In those days, the town was notorious for robberies, debauchery and violence, as it was far beyond the reaches of the law. So notorious was this town that it became the archetypal cowboy town in many Western movies.

One historical character stood out. Infamous among the bandits of Tombstone was a Chinese lady known as Mrs. Ah Lum or "China Mary." She hailed from Zhongshan county in China, and she was a very bold and resourceful woman. She was influential among the whites, and she controlled all the Chinese labour in the town. No Chinese person could be hired or paid except through China Mary. She owned an interest in most of the Chinese businesses there, while running her own general provisions store. Behind her store, she operated a gambling den that was open to both Westerners and Asians. On top of that, she controlled Chinese prostitution and all the opium trade in Tombstone. Mrs. Ah Lum was well-liked, respected and feared by all around her, regardless of their race or ethnicity. She lived to the ripe old age of 67 and her tomb remains well preserved.

We stood by her tomb as we took some photographs. Here laid an immigrant from China who thrived and succeeded alone in such a hostile environment. She was a truly remarkable woman, and her life story inspired us. If she could thrive so well in an alien land all by herself, so could we.

By afternoon, we arrived at Fort Huchuca, where we were welcomed with much pomp and ceremony. Standing before us were high ranking officers and the Mayor of the town. Standing opposite them were the honour guards of the Military Police carrying the various military standards. The ceremony started with a presentation of arms, and was followed by the playing of our Chinese national anthem by their military band. Standing ram-rod at attention, the atmosphere was most impressive, and quite stirring for us. As the stars and stripes of the American flag unfurled in the wind, the Colonel came forward and shook our hands with the warmest welcome.

We stayed for a sumptuous dinner, where the Colonel gave a rousing speech. He spoke about how the Americans and Chinese were able to work together for the common good, and how this was proof that we can continue working closely together into the future. What impressed us most was his knowledge of the situation in China. For someone who grew up in America, the Colonel's depth of knowledge of our culture, history, current affairs, and his sympathy to our plight under the Japanese occupation was just incredible. He possessed both understanding and insight, and he presented himself not as a superior, but as a kind friend who's always there for a friend in need.

* * *

15 April 1944

Douglas Air Field, Douglas, Arizona

There was much excitement in the air. There were crowds standing around the parade square. The military band was performing, filling the air with lively music. Today marks our first anniversary of joining the CAF, and more importantly, our graduation as full-fledged pilots.

Standing at the parade square were the graduating class of American and Chinese pilots. It was a huge honour for us Chinese to share the parade square with them. But it was also one that brought us sadness. Our American friends had brought their families, lovers, and friends to share in the celebration. But we had no one. Our families and friends are on the other side of the globe and could not witness our crowning moment.

The Commanding Officer came up to each one of us, pinned the wings onto our uniform, and presented us with a diploma for completing our training as pilots. We didn't just get our wings to fly as a certified pilot, we were also commissioned as military officers, and I was promoted to the rank of Sub-Lieutenant.

While standing at the parade square, I paused for a brief moment to reflect on my progress. It was incredible just how far I've come after so many months. What I have achieved thus far was one that filled me with great pride. For me, this was a memorable moment, and one that I wished my family could have witnessed. From this day on, I was a full-fledged bomber pilot, an officer of the CAF. It gave me a great sense of pride and satisfaction to know that I had passed all the stages of the very challenging flight training course.

Of the original class of 120 cadets, only 80 of us (two-thirds of the cohort) graduated as pilots. We were all proud of each other, and what we had achieved together. Though we didn't have our loved ones around to witness this momentous occasion, we still had each other.

We called this year of training a "miracle year" because we had completed an entire course of flying from a cadet to a certified pilot in twelve months without any disruption. Whether it was bad weather, lack of fuel, aircraft serviceability, or non-availability of flight instructors, we never missed a single day of flying.

When we started this "miracle year," we felt very lost and powerless. We wanted to do something for our country but we couldn't. And now, after travelling and training in far distant lands, we finally did it. We can now return to defend and protect our land.

The moment the ceremony ended, we warmly embraced each other. Full of emotion we broke out in patriotic song. We were ready to serve, we were ready to fly.

Chapter 12

SAD DEPARTURE

April 1944

La Junta Air Field, Colorado

Not long after our graduation and commissioning ceremony, twelve of us Chinese bomber pilots were posted to La Junta Air Field in Colorado for our final phase of training with the Operational Training Unit (OTU).

La Junta was a newly built military base, equipped with all the essential flight training facilities. It was huge, and many different types of bomber aircraft were stationed there, such as the B-25 Mitchells, the A-26 Havocs, and the heavy bomber B-24 Liberators.

We were very eager to begin our new phase of life at La Junta, as we learnt that our training involved the B-25 Mitchell medium bomber, which was the combat aircraft used in China. We were finally going to fly the real thing!

At La Junta, I was reunited with some of my mates who had dropped out of the earlier flight training phases. They had been trained for other flight programmes and were stationed here. It was a very happy reunion for me to meet many familiar faces.

Life at La Junta Air Base was a completely new 'ball game' for me. I had gone from cadet pilot to commissioned officer. As a newly minted pilot officer, I received a doubling of my pay from USD$60 to USD$120 a month, though this time, I had to cover the cost of my own meals. It was a huge relief to finally make officer rank as we were now provided with better quarters and entertainment facilities. Nonetheless, we were expected to keep our uniforms neat and exemplary at all times. And though we were only Sub-lieutenants, we attracted salutes from the enlisted ranks, and we were required to smartly return the salute. Life now was a lot more comfortable, and I must confess that the novelty of being an officer took a while to wear off.

We undertook a four-month conversion training to operate the B-25 Mitchell medium bomber aircraft. The aircraft had a far longer range, and had more power than anything we had flown up to this point. The B-25 Mitchell bombers were a challenge to fly, requiring great concentration and precise decision making. And for this reason, we had to re-learn many familiar procedures, such as take-off and landing, navigation, formation flying, instrument flying, long-range flights, and tactical manoeuvres, just to name a few. We also had to undergo special gunnery training as the B-25 bombers were armed with a powerful 75mm anti-tank M4 cannon.

***

As La Junta was a very small town with a big air base, it was very easy for us to come out to town when we needed time out and away from the base. Months of training had passed and we were nearing the end of our conversion training, so we had lots of free time to spare.

One day, I went out to town to grab a meal. I was dressed smartly in my uniform, and wherever I went, I was saluted because of my rank. This attracted the attention of a very pretty American girl. She had a petite frame and long blond hair flowing down her shoulders. Her smile was incredibly charming.

She came up to me, with her eyes gleaming bright. She had never met a Chinese man before. This was the first time she had encountered one, and for that matter, one dressed so splendidly in military uniform. She introduced herself as Marilyn Sweeney. She had just graduated from college with a long summer vacation ahead of her. Of all the women I met in my life, this is the first time I had encountered someone so bubbly and so full of life.

It was clear that she was very attracted to me. I too was very attracted to her. We had plenty of time to spare, and so we began dating. As our relationship progressed, I learnt more about her and her family. She was an only child living with her mother. Her father had passed away when she was young, and she lacked an older male figure. This might have explained her strong attraction to me when we first met. Nonetheless, our relationship flourished. We grew closer and closer, and Marilyn became quite attached to me.

As the weeks passed, my OTU training drew to a close. We faced a difficult dilemma about our relationship. In a few days' time, I had to leave America and return to China to fight the war. We would be separated and there's no guarantee that I would survive. No one knows how long this war will last. It would not be fair to Marilyn if she waited for my return, that is, if I survived. But even if we were to continue our relationship after the war, the harsh reality was that we come from two different backgrounds, two different cultures, two different ways of life. We had only been dating for less than a month. There's no guarantee that she'd be happy spending the rest of her life with me.

Marilyn, however, was a romantic and an idealist. She naively believed that love could overcome all adversities. She declared her love for me and that her love would not relent, saying, "I want to get married to you now!"

I was uncomfortable with her decision. I did not want to marry her because I could not guarantee that I would return to America after the war. Eventually, we came to a compromise. I bought her a ring and we got engaged, promising each other that we would wait until the end of the war before deciding what to do next. She was so happy that day. This helped to put her mind at ease.

* * *

September 1944

The dreaded day of separation had come. It was now time for me to leave her here in America, as I began my slow journey back to China. This being our last moment together, Marilyn accompanied me all the way to the railway station, her hand tightly grasping mine, every step of the way.

While waiting for the train to arrive, we talked about our hopes, our dreams, our possible future together when we meet again, and just how much we would miss each other. It was a difficult conversation. We didn't know what the future held for us. There was no certainty whether or not I would return. We could hardly hold back our feelings. Tears rolled down her eyes whenever she thought about the fact that we wouldn't be able to see each other again.

The train arrived at the station. As the doors of the carriages opened, people on the platform began bidding farewell to their loved ones. It was an emotional event. Of all the farewells that I bade whilst in America, this was the toughest. I reached out to hold Marilyn's hands, and grasped them tightly in mine. As I looked into her eyes, I promised her that I would call her every night. She accepted this promise and embraced me tightly for the last time.

The train conductor announced the last call to board the train. It was time for us to go our separate ways.

* * *

20 September 1944

Military Holding Station, Santa Ana, Orange County, California

I was amongst the twelve CAF pilots who boarded the train that day. While the other pilots were excited about returning to China, my mind was fixated on Marilyn. I could not stop worrying about her. There was very little I could do on the train that could take my mind off her. I kept wondering whether we had made the right decision to be engaged. Were we too young and foolish, too rash and imprudent about matters of love?

At Santa Ana, we settled down at a military holding station, where we waited for the ship that would bring us on a long voyage back to China. While I was there, I caught sight of something incredibly remarkable! There was a group of men dressed in prison garbs, marching across the square. And in that group, I saw a familiar face. I rushed out to get a closer look. It was Willy! I couldn't believe my eyes!

He turned his head in my direction and recognised me in the distance, and gave me the same calm smile and expression so typical of him. I approached the marching group as close as I dared, and asked him where they were marching to. He replied, "Why don't you come and see?"

So I followed them to a holding cell where military prisoners were locked up. As an officer, I was permitted to visit his cell. There, behind the bars, stood Willy as cool as ever, carrying himself with quiet dignity. It requires more than a disaster of this nature to shake his calm demeanour. He told me that he had found it difficult to earn a reasonable living in Mexico, so he tried to sneak back into the USA across the Rio Grande, where he was caught by the Military Police. He smiled as he told me this, as if he was just relating another one of his daring adventures. I had the feeling that he was tired of being a fugitive wandering about, and so he took a big risk, knowing there was a fair chance of being caught.

He was now waiting to be deported to China, and once there we both knew he would be tried, and upon a guilty verdict, summarily executed with a bullet in the head. I asked if there was anything I could do for him. And in his typical laconic style, he replied, "You could bring me a carton of Lucky Strike cigarettes." I was amazed at his positive attitude to life and his ability to be cheerful even in the most difficult of circumstances.

Before embarking on my voyage to China, I visited Willy a couple more times in his cell, bringing him the cigarettes he requested. Every visit was a bitter-sweet moment. I was happy to see a good friend once again and to engage in hearty discussions, and yet I felt so sad knowing the fate that awaited him. My heart ached each time I walked away, knowing that this is a friend that I will not see again.

* * *

We were not assigned any tasks at Santa Ana, except to wait for our boarding orders. So to pass the time, we decided to keep ourselves amused with the various attractions and entertainments.

Despite the many travels in and around the port city during my first two days there, I was able to keep my promise to Marilyn, calling her each night to talk about our day. I entertained her by telling her about all the things I did and saw in Santa Ana.

On the third day, I visited an American couple whom I met when I first arrived in America. They learnt that I was in California, and they invited me to their home in Pasadena (North-West of Santa Ana). I cooked dinner for them, and by the time we were done with dinner, it was already very late. It would have been a long drive back to Santa Ana, and so they warmly invited me to stay the night in their home. I obliged.

I was so preoccupied with the intense discussions I had with the couple that I had completely forgotten about my promise to Marilyn! By the time I realised, it was too late in the night. She was probably asleep. I guessed she must have been angry with me for breaking the promise. But I was hopeful that my call the next day would ease her anxieties of separation.

* * *

23 September 1944

Military Holding Station, Santa Ana, Orange County, California

The next day, I returned to Santa Ana and phoned Marilyn that evening as usual. I was startled by the voice I heard on the line. It was an unfamiliar female voice that sounded nothing like

Marilyn's or her mother's. As far as I knew, Marilyn did not have any friends or relatives staying with them.

"May I speak to Marilyn?", I asked.

The voice on the line identified herself as Marilyn's aunt, and she answered, "Marilyn has gone away."

Gone away? I was puzzled by the response. I was quite sure Marilyn would have told me if she was planning a trip. We spoke two evenings ago, and she was not the kind of person who would go on a last minute trip.

I was confused. Marilyn would not normally behave like this.

Was Marilyn upset with me for failing to call yesterday that she doesn't want to speak to me? Perhaps she got one of her friends to answer the phone.

I persisted in asking about Marilyn's whereabouts. The lady sounded like she was holding back her emotions.

"I'm sorry...", she said, "I'm sorry to tell you that Marilyn had just passed away."

I heard those words loud and clear, but my mind had so much difficulty comprehanding what I had heard. Marilyn's so young. And we were separated for only four days. She was in the pink of health when we parted. I couldn't believe it. I didn't want to believe it. If this was Marilyn's idea of a prank for getting back at me, this has certainly gone too far. I was so emotional and confused.

I demanded an explanation.

The lady explained that Marilyn passed away yesterday morning due to an asthma attack.

I was in total shock. I hung up the phone, feeling so completely lost. I did not know what to say or how I should feel about the news. It sounded too implausible. How could something like this happen to her?

When I felt calmer, I picked up the phone and called again. This time I asked to speak with Marilyn's mother. But she did not want to come to the phone. Was she too distraught to speak to me? Or was Marilyn's family trying to separate us?

The lady who identified herself as Marilyn's aunt told me that the funeral was in three days' time. Was this true? I needed to know. I had so many unanswered questions. Was Marilyn really gone for good? Or was this just a ploy for her family to keep us separated now that I had left Colorado?

I was so desperate for answers. I begged my commanding officer to let me return to Colorado. If she had indeed passed away, I could at least attend her funeral and send her off one last time. Otherwise, I would had at least some closure knowing that she's still alive.

Unsurprisingly, my commanding officer denied my request. The ship was arriving any day now, and I would miss the transport back to China. He sternly warned me not to go AWOL, and ordered soldiers to keep a close watch on me to make sure that I did not make a rash decision to return to Colorado.

I was at a loss, and I resigned myself to the fact that all I could do was to call Marilyn's home again to offer my condolences, and ordered a wreath of flowers to be brought to her funeral.

Was Marilyn alive or did she indeed pass away? I figured it was better to imagine that she had departed.

A day later, the ship arrived at the port. I boarded it with a very heavy heart. It was a sad departure.

Chapter 13

TROUBLED WATERS

October 1944

Pacific Ocean

The voyage back to China had been long and fraught with danger. By this stage of the war, the Japanese had occupied almost all of South East Asia, and had deployed their warships and submarines all across the Pacific Ocean. Each day out at sea exposed us to the possibility of meeting our demise much sooner than expected.

We felt quite helpless sitting on board this 'floating bathtub' otherwise known as the *S. S. Samuel G. French*, a merchant vessel serving the US military. There was nothing we could do to defend ourselves. We were just sitting ducks out in the open sea.

The thought of death constantly ran through the back of our minds. We kept ourselves busy to distract us from the dread of meeting the enemy.

I spent most of my time looking through the many photographs I took while in the United States, reminiscing the time I spent there with my friends, and most of all, with Marilyn. It was a bag of bittersweet memories, but I certainly cherished every single photograph in my collection.

I realised that as a photographer, every image I capture is more than a picture of people or the places I visited. When I capture an image of reality on film, I add a part of myself — my experiences, my ideals, my prejudices, and even my strength — into that picture. I become a part of the world I had travelled through, together with the people I meet along the way. What I chose to capture was a way for me to talk about an idea. Every photograph in my album forms a cross-section of the way in which I talk about my youthful days abroad. Regardless of what memory or emotion it evokes, each picture is itself an individual note, a recording of the people and places I met, and a song of my youth.

Looking through the photographs I took, I was amazed at how much I had grown over that one year. My naïve idealism had now been tempered by realism and painful loss.

* * *

On this voyage, I befriended a fellow passenger by the name of Mr. W. C. McCuller. I learnt that he too was struck with personal grief from having just lost his dear beloved mother. But life can be so cruel sometimes. Before Mr. McCuller could recover emotionally from the loss of his mother, he had to pack his bags and leave his hometown of Oakland, California, for his overseas military posting.

In many ways, we were quite blessed to have found each other on board the ship. If not for this chanced encounter, we would have had to shoulder the burden of our grief all alone for months on this ship full of strangers. But now, we didn't have to suffer alone. Our own personal grief enabled us to console each other and offer mutual support. It was through our conversations that we found the strength to recover from our loss.

* * *

17 November 1944

The Bay of Bengal

As we drew closer to India, our voyage on the Bay of Bengal became far more dangerous. If you looked out at the ocean, you might be deceived by the appearance of calm, peaceful waters. Yet, on closer inspection, you could see many patches of oil slicks and debris floating on the waters. Japanese submarines were very active in this part of the sea, and these were evidence of the woeful demise faced by our less fortunate allied ships. The sight brought us much dread.

Suddenly, there was a huge commotion on board the ship. Some of the crew had sighted a submarine in the distance. Did it belong to our allies, or was it the enemy's? There was no way to tell. The ship's alarm sounded, bringing everyone on board to a fever pitch of anxiety and fear. We were instructed to put on our helmets and prepare for the worst. Our ship was only a merchant vessel, it was not equipped to evade submarines, or any kind of counter-measure at all.

Everyone scrambled to their stations, ready for the fate that might await us. Some were so stricken with fear that they could not move. Others fell on their knees, deep in prayer for God's protection.

I rushed to strap the helmet on my head, closed my eyes, held my breath, and prayed like it was my last.

* * *

An hour had passed. Nothing happened. Two hours passed, and still nothing happened.

Perhaps the submarine did not spot us. Or if it did, it chose not to engage with us. By nightfall, we began easing up as it became clear that the threat of an attack was no more. However, I could see that many of us on board were still quite visibly shaken by the encounter. Very few of us could sleep soundly that night.

We continued our voyage without harassment from the enemy. Days later, we finally arrived at Calcutta, safe and sound, bringing our two-month long voyage to a close.

Chapter 14

MISSION ACCOMPLISHED

January 1945

Fourteenth Air Force Base, Hanzhong, Xi'an, China

In the early stages of the war, in 1938, the Japanese invaded Shanghai and Nanking, forcing the Kuomingtang (KMT) government to move inland into the mountainous region of Chungking in Sichuan Province. The Imperial Japanese Air Force had completely wiped out the inferior Chinese Air Force, and Chungking was consequently subjected to an endless array of Japanese aerial attacks.

Out of desperation, General Chiang Kai-shek sought the help of the United States, which sent aerial support to China in the form of American pilots and ground crew volunteers led by the charismatic, and rather unorthodox, General Claire Lee Chennault, of the First American Volunteer Group (AVG). They were essentially mercenary 'volunteer' pilots, paid for each aerial combat mission against the Japanese in their P-40 Warhawks.

After the Japanese attack on Pearl Harbour on 7 December 1941, the AVG was disbanded, and the remaining aircraft and crew were brought together to form the Fourteenth Air Force (a.k.a. the

'Fighting Fourteen'). And under the Lend-Lease agreement between China and the US, the US aided China through the provision of war material and training of Chinese forces, including the training of pilots in the US (which enabled me to be trained in my 'Miracle Year' in the US).

The 'Fighting Fourteenth' was made up of four wings. Three wings comprised either American or Chinese crews. The fourth wing, which I was posted to, the Chinese-American Composite Wing (CACW), comprised Chinese and American military personnel. The idea was to train the Chinese in a pragmatic environment, and to enable them to eventually take over command of the wing.

It was after a series of flights from Calcutta that I finally arrived in Hanzhong, where I was posted to the First Bombardment Squadron (or what we affectionately referred to as the First Bomb Squadron) of the Fourteenth Air Force, under the Chinese-American Composite Wing.

When I first joined the squadron, I had two commanders: Raymond L. Hodges who was the outgoing commander; and Richard Varney, who was learning the ropes from Hodges to take over the command of the squadron. They were both Americans and they were very brave heroes who fought against the Japanese during aerial missions to bomb the Yellow River Bridge in 1943. The bridge was key to the Japanese army, and the Japanese had fortified the bridge with many anti-air defences. There was a 50–50 chance of survival, and many American pilots lost their lives during that mission. The two commanders lived to tell the tale. Everyone in the squadron had the utmost respect for their bravery and leadership.

* * *

Life in Hanzhong was quite unlike the experience we had in the US. Situated right in the middle of a war, we had to settle quickly into squadron life, and we did our very best to adjust to the intense daily operational routines of the squadron. As officers, we felt like we had an extra burden to shoulder by virtue of our rank and responsibility, and we had to quickly learn who was who in the Chinese and American contingents.

The accommodation and food were reasonable, but it was nothing close to the pampered lifestyle we enjoyed back in the US. It was basic, but it provided us with a reasonable sanctuary of comfort and relaxation. Almost our entire existence centred on the airbase: we practically ate, slept, and socialised in the same compound.

While Hanzhong was our little sanctuary amidst the war, we couldn't help but live in constant fear that the enemy would launch a surprise attack against us. The threat of death was constantly dwelling at the back of our minds. As they say, an idle mind is the devil's playground. And under these circumstances, we knew that it was not healthy to allow any of our minds to go idle. We could easily breakdown from the stress of war. So we made it an effort to use every moment of our spare time to socialise. We organised many gatherings and spent our recreational hours playing basketball, tennis, singing, playing cards and, chatting about loved ones. All these helped to keep our minds distracted from the anxieties of war, and it helped foster a lively communal atmosphere, which forged deep and abiding friendships.

The combination of the crew from both countries was thought to be formidable and progressive, though language often was an obstacle that we had to deal with on a regular basis. Through our frequent interactions with each other, we overcame the language barrier through a hybrid language that was a mixture of both

English and Chinese, sprinkled with interesting hand gestures to make up for the lack of vocabulary. This was only possible because of the strong cohesive environment that we had developed from socialising and working on a daily basis. The hybrid language served us very well, proving once again necessity is the mother of invention.

* * *

Of all the friendships I forged in Hanzhong, I was closest to Howard Halla. Halla was an American bomber pilot who had been stationed in China for some time. He loved to share stories of how he fought alongside heroes like General Chennault, and Commanders Hodges and Varney, on so many dangerous missions. He was very proud of the fact that he participated in the bombing of the Yellow River Bridge in 1943 while recovering from jaundice, and survived!

We worked very closely together, and we were always looking out for each other. But more than just a friend, Halla became a close confidante and my godfather. He learnt that I had been baptised when the Japanese first invaded Hong Kong. But due to the war, I had received little direction pertaining to my own spiritual growth. He took the responsibility upon himself to educate and guide me in the faith.

Perhaps this was why Halla and I grew to become such close buddies. Beyond the experiences, memories and emotions that I shared with my many friends in Hanzhong, only Halla and I shared a deep spiritual bond that raised our hearts and minds beyond all earthly matters.

* * *

1 February 1945

A few weeks had passed, and by now many of us new pilots were itching to join the fight against the Japanese. We really wanted to show that we were capable and competent to perform the missions we spent so long training for. We were, after all, very proud of our wings, and eager to prove ourselves, and rid our land of the invaders.

Every evening during dinner time, the squadron clerk would pin up the roster for the next day's mission. This was the thing everyone in the squadron looked forward to each day. And we would often abandon our meals halfway just to search for our names on the roster. We knew the dangers that accompanied every mission, and we were well aware that we may not return. However, we were trained to fly, and there was an undeniable thrill to each experience.

For the past few weeks, we felt quite dismayed to find our names missing from the roster. There wasn't much for us to do. So we would often stand around our aircraft offering assistance to the ground crew. Sometimes, we would help them out with the aircraft preparation, safety checks, or with mundane tasks like organising the maintenance of equipment.

When other aircrews were rostered, we would wave them off at the dispersal area, and be there to welcome them home again. The local villagers would also cheer whenever they saw aircraft returning from a mission. It was a heart-warming sight to behold.

One evening, I got up from my seat to check the roster for the next day's mission. I was incredibly surprised to see my name on the roster for the first time. I was to be co-pilot to a very experienced, senior Chinese pilot. It was a reconnaissance mission involving two B-25 Mitchells, which were twin-engined medium-sized bombers, with five or six crew members comprising the pilot, co-pilot, radio operator, navigator, and dorsal and rear gunners. It was an extremely versatile aircraft which could operate at low and medium altitudes.

We were required to fly over an area a short distance away from our airbase to record the positions of the enemy. The moment the engines of my B-25 aircraft began rumbling, I could feel the adrenaline surging through my body. This was going to be the first time I would fly over the battlefield. It was a thrilling sensation.

What if they spotted us? Would they shoot us?

Our aircraft flew over the Japanese troops, and I duly recorded their positions. We returned to base without any incident, though to be honest, I felt somewhat disappointed that we returned to base without engaging the enemy, not even with harassing fire.

* * *

30 March 1945

Weeks later, I was sent on my second combat mission. This time, it was the "real thing," a strafing mission where we would attack enemy ground targets along the Nanyang Feng Cheng area by flying over them at a very low level. This was a risky operation, as we could get shot at such a low height. But we could not afford to be scared. Once you're scared, you cannot perform during the mission. I had to completely focus all my concentration on the task at hand.

Once again we operated in a pair, and we took turns to deliver two strafing runs at the enemy. On our first pass over them, we strafed the column of enemy cavalry, causing the horses to panic, throwing the troops off their mount. The horses ran away, and I could see enemy troops dispersing from the highway, attempting to take cover. We made a second pass over them to ensure that we eliminated them completely.

Our B-25 Mitchells flew so low over the ground, that I could see every vivid detail of the enemy troops. They were in a state of panic at the suddenness of the attack.

Each time I opened up the machine guns to fire at them, I told myself that this was for all the cruel and evil things they had done to China and to my compatriots. This was payback for all the horrible and wicked things — the rape, the torture, the murder — that they had done to my friends back in Hong Kong, and to everyone else in China.

I killed many enemy troops that day. It was cruel. It was war.

I had been waiting so long to fight against them after such a lengthy period of hardship and uncertainty as a student refugee. I felt that they deserved it for all the atrocities they had committed to my friends and to my fellowmen. And it felt so satisfying to exact vengeance after such a long time.

I was so completely absorbed in the mission that I forgot about my fears of being shot down. At one point, enemy fire damaged the fuselage of my plane. But I was not worried at all. There was no anxiety, no dread, no fear of death. The surge of adrenaline and the satisfaction of finally being able to fight against the invaders overwhelmed my entire being. I was like a different person. I was completely unafraid.

***

27 April 1945

I was excited about my third combat mission. This time, we had to attack a target at the Yellow River Bridge. The entire squadron was sent, with six B-25 aircraft flying in formation.

Along the way, we discovered a faulty flight indicator on our aircraft. We could not risk losing our highly specialised crew members because of a technical fault. It was not worth the risk. We had no choice but to abort the mission and return to base.

War has a powerful effect on uniting our psyches. Amongst the aircrew, every one of us felt connected to each other, as if we were one. When our faulty aircraft had to return to base, everyone else on the mission felt our disappointment. And when we waited back at base for the other aircraft to return, those of us on the ground felt the same sense of elation whenever we saw the other aircraft return safely. We saw just how extensive the damage was to the aircraft that returned. There were dozens of shrapnel holes in urgent need of patching up. We felt the same worry that the aircrew felt as they struggled to make their way back alive. And upon hearing news of a successful mission, we all felt the same sense of satisfaction as if we were the ones who had gone on that mission.

This was a very special bond that we pilots shared with each other. This brought us close together as fellow brothers-in-arms.

* * *

3 May 1945

My fourth mission was known as a "twin operation," where two or more bombers were escorted by more agile fighter planes to the target area. The P-51 Mustang fighter planes would nip in quickly and drop smaller bombs to first suppress the anti-aircraft defences. Then our medium B-25 bombers would proceed to bomb "the hell out of the targets." It was generally safer for us in the B-25s, as we were much higher up in the air, and less exposed to enemy flak.

Occasionally, we would swoop down to join in low-level strafing with the P-51 fighter planes. This was all coordinated by radio intercom, but it was difficult to do so as the B-25 was a very noisy plane.

Yet, despite the noise, we were able to coordinate the operation effectively, and the incendiary bombing was a success. We managed to destroy an enemy supply dump in the Nanyang area.

* * *

4 June 1945

This was my fifth combat mission, and it was a big one. The entire squadron was activated to attack a railway yard in Sin Siang City. This was a high-level bombing mission, and it required bombers to fly in formation, ready to drop a payload of 3000 lbs (1.4 tonnes) of bombs, that would do massive damage to the enemy target. Once again, the agile P-51 fighter planes would lead the way to protect the lumbering bombers from enemy fighter attacks.

The railway yard was a vital enemy installation, and was an obvious target for such bombing missions. The Japanese had fortified the area with many anti-aircraft guns.

Unfortunately for us, there was a sand storm during the operation, making it almost impossible to fly in formation. Not only that, we encountered heavy enemy fire from the ground. There were many casualties that day.

It was very upsetting to witness a nearby aircraft hit by enemy flak. On one hand, I had to struggle with the thought that it could have been me. On the other hand, I knew that inside that plane, one or more of my friends were killed by the flak, or that they would die a very painful death the moment the aircraft hit the ground.

Whenever this happened, we had no choice but to continue flying. We had a mission that we needed to accomplish. And most important of all, as pilots, we had to take care of our own crew and return safely to base.

We were not supposed to let our emotions affect us, but it was difficult. Our special bond as brothers-in-arms meant that we could all feel the same sense of anguish and pain. There and then, in the cockpit, in the heart of battle, we had to accept the loss of our friends and stoically continue the mission as if nothing had happened.

Our wing has a tradition where we would hold a big celebration for those who made it back to base that day. Sometimes, it can be difficult to overcome the loss of our friends, and we had to constantly distract ourselves with such celebrations, or keep ourselves busy with other activities like movies or sports. We had to stay strong in order to move on.

Losing a fellow brother in battle was hard. What was even more difficult was the ritual of personally breaking the news to families of the deceased. I had to accompany my commander to the homes of three of my fallen brothers.

Dressed smartly in our military uniform, we knocked on the door of their parents' homes. My commander would hand them a set of uniform once worn by their deceased son, apologise, and recount the story of how he heroically lost his life in battle. It was excruciatingly painful to break the news, and then witnessing the elderly parents of your departed brother and friend fall to the ground, weeping in anguish at the loss of their son.

War was already bad enough. To lose one's beloved son whom they had spent years raising with love and tender devotion was worse.

Their departed son, their only source of hope for struggling to survive the war, was gone.

I felt an immense sorrow for them, but I didn't say anything to offer them comfort.

I couldn't. I was at a loss for words.

* * *

18 July 1945

This day marks my seventh combat mission. The sixth mission occurred fourteen days ago, but it was a failure due to bad weather. And so this was a second attempt at the same enemy target, a railway yard in Shijiazhuang, an area west of Beijing.

More than a month had passed, and I still had not gotten over the loss of my friends. But we had no choice but to continue fighting. After our first failed attempt, the enemy knew that we would try again a second time, and had strongly fortified their defences with more anti-aircraft guns. Once again, the entire squadron was activated, and out we went in full force, dropping bombs on the enemy target. This time, the mission was a success, though the wings of my aircraft were damaged by anti-aircraft guns. By the time I returned to base, my B-25 aircraft had several holes that needed patching up.

Half a year had passed, and it's difficult to say whether I have gotten used to warfare. It was still very nerve-wrecking. The hard part about it all was losing my friends in battle. One moment you're laughing with them. The next moment, they're gone. There's rarely even a body to bid farewell to. All that's left are photographs of them, and the material possessions they left behind in the airbase. Much harder still is to enter a room and feel their absence in our midst. It gets increasingly more difficult to get through the day with every friend I lose.

* * *

11 August 1945

Liangshan Airfield, Chongqing Province

Immediately after my eighth combat mission to destroy a railway yard in Suzhou, our entire wing was ordered to assemble in a base called Liangshan, near the Yangtze River. This was to be the biggest air combat operation to date, and it involved all the bombardment squadrons of the Fourteenth Air Force to carry out bombing raids over Shanghai. We were very excited by the scale of the operation, and we met many pilots who flew in from airbases all across China.

By this time, however, we began hearing rumours about a Japanese surrender. We were aware that the Imperial Japanese forces occupying China were gradually shrinking as their troops, aircraft, and supplies were diverted to fend off increased attacks by the US and the Allied forces in the Pacific. But the idea that the Japanese would surrender so soon seemed to us quite implausible.

It was time for us to begin preparation for the operation. I was thrilled at the idea of such a large-scale attack. I was more than ready to embark on my ninth mission.

But before any of us could board our aircraft, the commander of the operation gave the order to abort the mission. We were all very confused.

Hours later, the commander broke the news that the rumours were indeed true. The Japanese were making preparations for surrender, and there was no need to carry out any further attacks.

We had very mixed feelings about the news. Yes, it was good news. But it was news that came sooner than we had expected. Some felt that the Japanese had surrendered too early. Some others felt they had surrendered too late. Regardless of how we felt about the surrender, we were relieved by the news.

The war was finally over.

Chapter 15

CIVIL WAR

Wang Jia Dun Hankou Airfield, Hubei Province

Since the Japanese surrendered, life in the airbase changed drastically overnight. The ever-constant worry of a surprise attack vanished immediately into thin air. The tense atmosphere had relaxed into one of serenity and calm. There was no enemy, no more danger, no anxiety or the fear of death. We did not have to worry about losing any of our brothers-in-arms at the next flight, no need to worry about causing immense grief to our parents if we were killed in action.

China was finally liberated, and we are now free! Life was now very relaxed, and every evening, we could go out for a night of entertainment and celebration.

Now that the war was over, it was time for the Americans to pass the baton over to the Chinese. They had helped to rebuild the China Air Force (CAF) after the Japanese had destroyed it, and now it was our turn to get it in order.

The American military had no further reason to stay in China. And as the weeks went by, our American brothers-in-arms began packing for their return back home. At the same time, the First Bomb Squadron, which I was a part of, was moved to a base in Hankou. Once again, it was another round of sad goodbyes as we parted ways.

At Hankou, we joined other Chinese bomber pilots, many of whom were far more senior and experienced than I was. In their eyes, I was very young and still fresh out of training. But they could see that I was keenly interested in doing more than the basic routine, so they roped me in to become a flight instructor. It was a crash course one-day training, as I already knew how to fly a B-25 Mitchell. All I needed to learn were the procedures crucial for an instructor, and to assure them that I was ready to train the new pilots.

Not too long after, a new batch of CAF pilots returned from their 'Miracle Year' training in the US. Ten of them were bomber pilots, and they were posted here to Hankou. As freshly minted pilots, they were very keen to fly. And as their newly-appointed instructor, I was very happy to give them the flight training they desired. These new pilots already knew the basics of flying, but they needed a refresher course as they had not flown for almost three months due to the long voyage back. Moreover, the aircraft that here was different from the ones used in the US. Here, the B-25s were heavier as they were equipped with a variety of war equipment and guns.

The training course comprised eight sessions over a span of two weeks. On each flight, I would bring two or three pilots into the cockpit at a time. Inside the cockpit, I would show them the ropes on how to manoeuvre the aircraft. On the first visit into the cockpit, I would instruct them while the aircraft was on the ground. On subsequent sessions, I taught them while we were up in the air. Once I could see that they had become confident in manoeuvring the aircraft, I let them fly solo.

The good thing about training them in peacetime was the fact that I had plenty of time to take care of them, and to ensure they properly mastered the fundamentals. It was a very meaningful and personal experience that allowed me to forge many close friendships. This was a luxury I could not enjoy when I arrived in China as a freshly minted pilot, due to the urgencies of war.

I was lucky to become good friends with two of my "students." One was Soong Han Ling, whom we affectionately called, "Honey" Soong. The other was Jimmy Wang. Over the course of our training, we got along very well and became good buddies. We enjoyed each other's company, and so we often went out to visit the many different night spots in town for a relaxing evening.

Over time, we became particularly drawn to a certain café featuring Hawaiian music and impromptu dances. This was a very new experience for the three of us, and we enjoyed it greatly.

We eventually became acquainted with two sisters, Augusta and Alberta Rodrigues. Born and raised in Shanghai, the sisters were here in Hankou to visit their aunt and uncle. This Hawaiian-themed café was the product of the sisters' creative minds to improve the café's business. The sisters themselves were very charming and friendly, and they breathed life into the café. Each night the two would perform a variety of Hawaiian songs. This was refreshing for us as almost every place we knew sang the same old Chinese songs. When they were not performing, we had a wonderful time chatting with them.

We enjoyed our time in the café so much that visits to the café became a regular evening routine, to such an extent that Honey, Jimmy, and I, became very good friends with the sisters as well.

Life was good.

* * *

While many of us were beginning to enjoy the newfound peace after the surrender, a new threat began to emerge.

Previously, the Kuomintang (KMT) led by Chiang Kai-shek and the Communists led by Mao Zedong had been fighting a common enemy. But now that war was over, the Communists wanted to play a bigger role in the development of China. The Communists proposed to work together with the KMT, but Chiang was reluctant to have anything to do with them. Despite several attempts at negotiating for peace, the two parties often clashed with each other.

To make matters worse, corruption was brewing in many parts of China. The KMT warlords had returned to their provinces and did their own thing, often contrary to what the KMT wanted. If you wanted to get somewhere, you had to pay your way through. The moral decay grew rampant like a tumour. Life after the war did not improve, and the plight of the poor only got from bad to worse.

As a consequence of this, many grew disillusioned with the KMT government. On the other hand, the Communists demonstrated that they were by the people for the people, and came to the material aid of many living in abject poverty. Support for the Communists and the Peoples' Liberation Army (PLA) grew rapidly, and their ideology spread like wildfire across the land. And despite the great military strength of the KMT (with the additional support from the USA), the PLA had grown so strong militarily that they began winning many battles, and started taking over parts of China.

China was plunging back into war, but this time, it was a war with herself.

* * *

By the summer of 1946, I started hearing rumours of combat missions against the Communists in China. As far as I was concerned, the war was over. I had joined the China Air Force to fight against the Japanese, and they had been defeated. It was one thing to conduct flight training. It was another thing altogether to fight in a war that I myself did not subscribe to. I had been fighting to protect my fellow Chinese compatriots from an oppressive invader. And now, the thought of having to kill the very people I had been defending — that to me was unconscionable, and I wanted nothing to do with it.

Life could not present a more gruesome and objectionable prospect, and this was precisely what I would be required to do if I chose to remain with the CAF.

I did my utmost best to avoid participating in any combat missions against the Communists. At first, I was able to limit my flying duties to conducting reconnaissance flights over Communist positions. Since these did not involve any bloodshed, they were the only missions I was willing to be involved in.

As time went on, the Communists gained a strong foothold over many parts of China, and the KMT, with their superior military force, knew that they had to quickly put the Communists down before they could grow any further in strength.

Once again, we were at war.

It became increasingly difficult to avoid combat missions against the Communists. And more and more pilots grew just as unhappy fighting against our fellowmen.

I knew that sooner or later, I would be forced to fight in the war that I did not subscribe to. It was simply against my principles. Yet,

I was confronted with a difficult dilemma, one that had no apparent solution: the CAF would not allow anyone to resign during such times of emergencies.

After many sleepless nights of deliberation, I finally thought of an idea. Perhaps I could apply for an extended leave of absence to visit my family back in Ipoh, Malaya. I had not seen them since 1941. I was confident that this was the perfect excuse to avoid fighting in the impending civil war, while I planned my next move.

I had absolutely no intention of returning to China to fight against the people I once defended.

I took my chances, filled up the leave application form, and submitted it to my commanding officer.

Chapter 16

THE GIFT

Days later, I received the greatest surprise. The CAF granted me a leave of absence without an expiry date! This meant that I was under no obligation to return to fight for the KMT. I was unsure if this was the result of an odd administrative error, or if my commanding officer was sympathetic to my moral objection and pulled some strings for this to happen. Whatever it was, this was my ticket out of this civil war.

I was elated, and I began packing my bags in preparation to leave China. During this time, I received word from a dear friend of mine that she was getting married. Her name was Loretta Ng-Quinn, and we were close friends back in Hong Kong University.

I first met her when we were riding on the same bus to campus. I sat across her and I was charmed by her graceful presence. We did not speak that day, but I later discovered that we were both classmates in the Arts Faculty. It was then that I got to know her better. Loretta was a sweet and charming young lady, full of zest for life. What I found most fascinating was just how well we clicked together. We had the same mind on many matters, and we shared the same aspirations.

The war made us closer friends as we worked together to help our friends. Loretta's grand palatial home was a safe-haven from Japanese intrusion. Her father, a lawyer, held a very high status that the Japanese did not dare mess with him. We gathered many of our friends to her home. It was the one place where we could speak freely without fear. And it was there that we poured out our frustrations and planned our escape out of Hong Kong. It was for this reason that we spent a lot of time together, not as lovers, but as close platonic friends. Unfortunately, we were separated after successfully fleeing to China. Loretta went up to Chengdu, while I went to Pingshi.

I was very much overjoyed to hear from Loretta once again, and happy to hear about her good news. I was about to leave China, and was unsure whether I would be able to return for her wedding. I had to meet her in person to give her a wedding gift.

***

It had been almost three years since we last saw each other. This long-awaited meet was something I looked forward to with great excitement. Yet, for days I agonised over what might have been a meaningful gift to her. I had nothing to give her.

In the end, I found the answer. It was a gift that was both practical and one that was profoundly meaningful even for myself.

I carried this gift concealed in a mysterious green bag, on my back and travelled all the way to her home in Shanghai to meet her.

Loretta opened her door to greet me. So much has happened, so much has changed over the course of three years. Yet, standing there at the entrance was the same sweet and charming young lady I remembered spending so much time in lively discussions back in Hong Kong. She was still full of life, so full of passion in her demeanour.

After spending many hours in heartfelt conversation, it was time for me to present her with the gift. I got up from my seat, strapped the mysterious bag on my back, and stood on the chair. Loretta stood before me, unsure of what to expect.

Looking at her, I said, "This is my gift to you." At those words, I pulled the ripcord attached to the mysterious bag.

In an instant, a huge white silky fabric shot out from the top of the bag, almost like a white rose blossoming at rapid speed. My gift to Loretta was my personal parachute which I used throughout my career in the CAF. I explained the significance and purpose of the parachute to her.

This parachute meant a lot to me. I carried it with me on every single flight since I was a cadet and on every dangerous mission during the war. No pilot ever went on a flight without one. And if a pilot were to ever give his personal parachute to someone else, it would be in the context of a pilot choosing to give up his life so that someone else might live.

I was quite fortunate never to have used the parachute before. Nonetheless, it was the one thing that gave me peace of mind that everything will be fine even if my aircraft was about to crash. It was for me both an instrument and symbol of safety and protection.

As I was preparing to leave the CAF, I had no need for it anymore. I had originally intended to keep it with me as a precious keepsake. But I decided that Loretta would benefit from it greatly. War had driven up the cost of textiles to the point that many could not afford it. Weddings are supposed to be joyful occasions. They should never be a source of financial anxiety and sadness. My parachute was white and made entirely of silk. It was the perfect material for the one friend who would be the perfect bride on her wedding day.

Loretta was overwhelmed with emotion, shedding tears of joy. She accepted the gift and thanked me for it.

* * *

January 1947

Ipoh, Malaya

My return to Ipoh was a huge surprise. The entire town welcomed me back, and gave me the treatment equivalent to that of a war hero. I felt like a victorious Roman general taking his triumphal march through the throngs of the Roman citizenry. It was so wonderful to see my family again after almost six years. My father, needless to say, was very proud of his son who had flown bombers in fights against the Japanese.

Once the fanfare over my return had fizzled out, I began devoting time to serious considerations about my future. The many years spent overseas had changed my outlook in life. As a pilot, I wanted to be airborne once again, but there was no such opportunity available back in Malaya. Not only that, my own definition of what I call "home," had changed. Yes, I grew up in Malaya with my family, but this was not my home. Not anymore.

When I was fleeing danger as a refugee, China embraced me and made me a citizen. When I chose to fight and liberate her from foreign aggression, she gave me wings to fly. I felt like I truly belonged, and I felt proud to call China my home.

Despite my refusal to fight in the civil war, I had a strong longing to return to this newfound home. My extended leave of absence from the CAF meant that I was not obliged to work for the KMT. I started exploring options and soon discovered that there was a lot that I can do to help restore this war-ravaged country. Thousands of people had fled the Japanese to the central regions of China, and they were stranded with nowhere to go. They needed help to be repatriated.

I began looking for opportunities to join a commercial airline that was already helping these people.

Chapter 17

ONE LOVE GAINED, ONE LOVE LOST

July 1948

Mukden Airport, Mukden, China

I stood by the tarmac to observe the chaos that was happening around me. Strewn along the tarmac were numerous furniture and bags of personal belongings that had been left behind. Peeking through the window into Mukden Airport, I could see a sea of people, every one of them with worried looks on their faces as they desperately waited to be evacuated to safety. There were many wounded KMT soldiers there too, and they were joined by many of Manchuria's elites, from the children of generals to officials of the KMT.

Manchuria was beginning to fall into the control of the Peoples' Liberation Army, and they were supported by many of the peasants who were disillusioned with suffering in poverty while the elites around them enjoyed a life of luxury.

It's been more than a year since I began flying for the Central Air Transport Corporation (CATC). At first, the flights I conducted were passenger flights to transport displaced persons back to their homes, or to transport freight supplies and building materials inland for the reconstruction of China. However, as the months went by, the civil war between the KMT and the Communist had intensified. Now, I was required to fly three times a day to evacuate people out of Manchuria to Beijing, which was a safe stronghold from the Peoples' Liberation Army.

Upon landing my plane, the ground crew were busily loading the personal possessions of many of the wealthy elites. Many of them were so attached to their material possessions, that they had their servants carry all the furniture out from their homes. There were bed frames, mattresses, sofas, and tables. The elites were attempting to load as much as they possibly could. Whatever possessions they could not salvage had to be abandoned on the tarmac.

I personally thought that this was just ridiculous. Lives are far more important than furniture. We could have evacuated more people to safety if we didn't have to transport all these bulky cargo. But these elites were wealthy paying customers, and as a transport pilot, I had to oblige.

* * *

September 1947

Shanghai

The head office of the CATC was based in Shanghai. When I first began work there, I learnt that Augusta and her family had relocated to Shanghai. I made it a point to reconnect with her and to renew our friendship. She received me courteously, though she was a little cold towards me. I later learnt that while I was away in Ipoh, Augusta had developed a relationship with another man by the name of Lucky, who was an air navigator for the China Air Force. She was very happy in her relationship and was very loyal in her love for him.

Months later, Lucky, was unfortunately transferred to work in Xi'an. The two tried to maintain a long distance relationship through regular letter-writing. But the civil war had disrupted postal services, making it difficult for them to correspond regularly with each other. As time went on, they eventually grew apart from each other.

Whenever I was in town, I made it a point to visit Augusta. She was one of the few friends I knew living in Shanghai. As months went by, she began to warm up towards me.

* * *

December 1947

Nanjing East Road, Shanghai

One day, while I was walking down the busy streets of Shanghai, I spotted a woman with a very familiar likeness from a distance. She was a small petite girl dressed in a *qipao* (traditional Chinese dress), with two pigtails tied on the sides of her head, and she looked incredibly studious. She reminded me of a very special someone whom I used to be close to almost ten years ago back in Ipoh.

I was unsure if she was the right person. It's hard to imagine that anyone would remain looking exactly the same after so many years. What were the odds that I would meet someone from Ipoh here in the busy streets of Shanghai?

I had to know. I haven't had contact with her after so many years. It was a chance I was not willing to pass. So I followed her from a distance, hoping to get a closer look at her. Eventually, I followed her into a bookshop and got a chance to see her up close.

I could not believe my eyes! I called out to her just to be sure, "Sook Fun! Is that you?"

She turned and responded. It really was her!

* * *

My friendship with Chong Sook Fun traced all the way back to our early years in Ipoh. I first got to know her through her friends. Sook Fun was educated in a Chinese school, and then became an educator at the same school. She wanted to learn English but had limited opportunities to do so. This led our common friends to introduce her to me, and I was very happy to oblige as I too wanted to improve my command of the Chinese language. So I became her English tutor, and she in turn became my Chinese tutor.

Sook Fun was more than a master of the Chinese language. She was very knowledgeable about China's history and current affairs. She took great pride in enlightening me all about China, and I enjoyed this very much as she opened my mind to a world of ideas that were once quite alien to me. Sook Fun was matured in her thoughts on political affairs. She found that I was always "sitting on the fence" on so many important matters, and attributed that behaviour to my "Western" education. And so she took it upon herself to educate me about the turmoil in China, and how China could one day progress as a nation.

Naturally, I was quite fascinated by her sharing. And I guessed she herself enjoyed sharing these things with me too. Over time, our meetings became more frequent, and we began sharing our feelings more openly with each other. Our friendship gradually blossomed into one of romance.

Sook Fun was the first girl I fell in love with, and being the young lovebirds that we were, we shared an exciting romantic relationship.

One fine day in 1938, a performance troupe from China, known as the Guo Wu Tuan, came to perform in Ipoh. They were travelling around South East Asia to rally support from overseas Chinese in the war effort against Japan. At Sook Fun's suggestion, we attended the concert.

Little did I realise that that was the concert that led to our separation. Sook Fun had been so roused up by the performance that she decided to become a journalist to assist in the war effort in China.

A few days after the performance, she ended our relationship and left Ipoh. That was the last I saw of her.

* * *

December 1947

Nanjing East Road, Shanghai

I could not believe my eyes! It was incredible that we could meet after all these years and in such unexpected circumstances. She was still the same scholarly girl that I knew. She had only walked into the bookshop, and yet she was already hugging several books in her arms.

I invited her out for a drink to catch up on old times, and she happily consented.

We settled down at a nearby café, which gave both of us a chance to take a proper look at each other. It's amazing just how little she had changed since we last met. I was mesmerised by her appearance: it was as if she hadn't changed one bit since the day she left Ipoh.

I noticed, however, that she did not look as happy as I was. She realised I was wearing my KMT China Air Force uniform, and began frowning in displeasure at the fact that I had joined the KMT. She berated me for wearing the KMT uniform, as she expressed contempt for Chiang Kai-shek and the KMT. In her opinion, they lacked compassion and failed to understand the plight of the people. The KMT was just a corrupt group driven by people with petty ambition, unlike the Communists, whose inspirational leaders gave the people a new impetus to change society for the better. She ended her tirade, saying, "The next time I see you, I don't wish to see you wearing this uniform."

The conversation reminded me of the time when we were together back in Ipoh, and how she had repeatedly emphasised my political naivety and ignorance. I used to admire her for being an intellectual over such matters. But not this time. I was not the same boy that I was ten years ago. I had grown so much over the years, and had my own stand on these matters. I too was starting to become disillusioned with Chiang Kai-shek for his weak leadership, yet I was diametrically opposed to her philosophy. The situation was a lot more complex, and it was not one that could have been easily resolved just by picking a side. There was so much more at stake. Besides, I was proud to wear the uniform because of how hard I fought to liberate China from Japanese aggression. It had nothing to do with the KMT.

Before we left the café, I tried to exchange contact details with Sook Fun. It was a strange moment as she gladly accepted mine but refused to share hers with me. I didn't put much thought to it then. I was just so happy to be reunited with her once again.

＊＊

Sook Fun and I continued to meet whenever I was in town. As she had my contact details, she was always the one initiating the meet-ups. Over the few conversations that we shared, I realised just how different we had become. Despite her small petite frame, she had a feisty personality, brimming with a strong disdain for the ruling KMT government. She was more radical than the person I knew in our younger days. I used to admire her for admonishing me for being so ignorant and naïve. Now, I was not so ignorant about such matters. I certainly did not enjoy being told off for my views on politics.

Perhaps there was a nostalgic part of me seeking to bring our friendship back to the good old romantic days. I found myself trying too hard to please her, even to the extent of not wearing my KMT uniform when meeting her. I had to pretend to be someone other than myself. I was unhappy.

As the civil war intensified, my work took me out of Shanghai more frequently. Whenever I returned to Shanghai, I found myself more inclined to spend those precious pockets of my free time with Augusta. We had spent a lot of time together and had grown quite close, and I started calling her Gus as a term of endearment.

I enjoyed spending time with Gus. At least when I was with her, I did not have to please her by pretending to be someone I was not. We were very comfortable being ourselves to each other. Naturally, we grew closer and our friendship blossomed into romance.

We were deeply in love with each other. I could not stop thinking about her. This was especially so whenever I was away on work trips. Each time I thought of her, I grabbed the nearest piece of paper I could find — whether it was a blank piece of paper, an unused application form, a receipt — and penned my thoughts to her. I sent her at least one love letter for every day that I was separated from her.

Gus was my inspiration and my muse. I penned this poem when I thought of her while flying from Hankou to Nanjing:

"We get out of Life
just what we put into it.
If we want happiness.
we must first learn to make others happy:
If we want love and kindness,
we must first give devotion and affection.
Nothing can hurt us save only as we let it.
Each failure brings us nearer to success
if we but profit by our mistakes.
A lot of people seem to think
the greatest accomplishment in this world
is to live it without work."

Gus was the love of my life, and she meant everything to me. After all that we had been through, I decided to make a commitment to her.

On 20 April 1948, I returned excitedly to Shanghai, headed straight from the airport to her home with a bouquet to flowers in one hand and a ring in another. I proposed, and she accepted. We were officially engaged that day.

* * *

September 1948

Shanghai

Shanghai was a very important international financial centre that brought together people from all walks of life. The KMT government was well-aware that Shanghai had been infiltrated by an underground group of Communists, but they didn't have the means to identify and catch them. It was only on rare occasions that they were able to catch individuals circulating pro-Communist propaganda. The KMT's had no tolerance for them, and they were swiftly executed for their actions.

The civil war had brought about hyperinflation. Food supplies into Shanghai were also disrupted, resulting in scarcity. Not too long ago, a fat stack of cash could once lavishly feed a person three times a day for an entire month. Now, it was worth so little, the same stack of cash could only buy a single bowl of noodles.

The underground Communists took advantage of the situation to fan the flames of discord. There were many uprisings in town. In response, the KMT government in Shanghai, led by Chiang Kai-shek's own son, ruled with an iron fist, imposing martial law on the town. He brought in the army to patrol the streets of Shanghai alongside the police. There was a curfew at night, and everyone's movement was restricted. You could not simply walk from one place to another as you pleased.

Yet, despite these restrictions, I was surprised that Sook Fun was able to move around very freely to meet me. It finally dawned on me that she had joined the underground Communists and became one of their agents. Her radical ideas, her hatred for the KMT, her refusal to share about her personal life or the means to contact her, and her ability to move around Shanghai so freely despite all the restrictions. She had to have special connections to get around those restrictions. I had no doubt that she helped to blow the cinders that grew into a raging fire of chaos that Shanghai was now engulfed in.

Here I was sitting face to face with the "enemy." Well, when she saw me in my KMT uniform at the beginning of our reunion, it was clear to her that I was on the wrong side. And all these while, she was pretending to be someone she was not, just as how I was pretending to be someone I was not just to please her. There was nothing genuine or sincere about these meetings we had. It was all a farce. Our reunion was a reunion built on lies.

I kept my cool, yet deep down, I was hurt. I felt betrayed by someone whom I used to love. The days of our youth were just a far distant memory, never to be recovered. We had grown too far apart from each other.

At the end of our meet, I announced to Sook Fun that I had just got engaged to Gus. And with that, we went our own separate ways.

Chapter 18

FLIGHT OF REFUGE

5 May 1949

Church of Christ the King, Shanghai

As the months went by, large parts of China fell to the Communists. By the end of 1948, the Peoples' Liberation Army had surrounded Beijing, the birthplace of the KMT and the internationally recognised capital of China. Despite strong resistance and military support from the Americans, the PLA successfully stormed the city of Beijing. This was a huge symbolic blow to the KMT, and one that cost many lives. Morale had sunk to an incredible new low.

Everyone in Shanghai was baffled by what had happened. We could not understand how such a defeat was even possible. The KMT had military and technological superiority, and was aided by foreign support. How could they have been defeated so easily? Once Beijing fell, many other cities toppled in quick succession, one after the other like dominoes.

A few months back, I was roped in to provide air support to General Yuan Shisan in the city of Taiyuan. General Yuan was a famous and powerful general with a formidable army. But Taiyuan was an isolated location, and his army was surrounded by the enemy forces who had cut off all ground supply lines. I had to fly over Taiyuan to airdrop essential supplies three times daily. This was the least we could do in an attempt to save them. But it was a futile effort. A few days later, the Communists defeated General Yuan and took over control of Taiyuan.

The PLA had conquered most of the northern parts of China, and now they were heading southwards toward the other capital city of Nanjing and to Shanghai. They had become such a formidable force that the KMT officials began relocating to Taiwan. News of the KMT's move to Taiwan was depressing. It was a signal that defeat was inevitable. Millions more began evacuating.

It was against this backdrop of war and chaos that the sounds of church bells rang. Gus and I put our worries aside for a brief moment to get married. It was a simple ceremony, attended by a handful of people. Most of our friends had already fled the city.

The battle for Shanghai was beginning to draw near. Despite the sounds of church bells resonating in the air, we could faintly hear fighting in the distance. We knew we had to evacuate out of Shanghai eventually. Nonetheless, the marriage ceremony was a joyous occasion for us, one that provided us with some relief from the persistent fear and dread of what was to come.

We vowed that we would be bound closely to each other, no matter what happens, in both good times and bad.

* * *

18 May 1949

I had just returned from yet another thirteen-day long operation to evacuate refugees out to safety. I was reluctant to do so, as I needed to fly out of Shanghai on the very day of my wedding. But if I didn't fly, who will evacuate those refugees? As it was, the major Chinese airlines were overstretched with such humanitarian work. They needed all the help they could get. I certainly did not like having to leave my precious Gus behind in Shanghai, especially not when the Communists were already fighting to enter the city.

I had a hard time concentrating while flying. I could not help but worry constantly about Gus. Every waking moment, I prayed very hard for her safety. When I wasn't in the air, my ears were glued attentively to the radio as I listened to the news updates about the civil war.

The moment I got out of the airport, I got into a jeep and drove straight to Gus' home. I had already briefed her that we would leave Shanghai the minute I returned. I arrived in the evening, and Gus was all packed and ready to go. Without any hesitation, we loaded our essential belongings into the jeep, and started making our way to the Longhua Airport.

The plan was to board the first flight out of Shanghai to Hong Kong at the crack of dawn. But Shanghai was still under martial law and the curfew made it impossible for us to get to the airport so early in the morning. This left us with no choice but to spend the night at the airport.

We arrived at the Longhua Airport very late into the night, and settled down in the CATC office. It was impossible to get any sleep.

Under the cover of darkness, the Communists began a massive attack on the city. Every few minutes, we could hear the screeching sounds of artillery shells raining down from the sky and the loud explosions that followed.

Will the airport be affected? Will we be captured? Will an artillery shell drop on us? These thoughts raced through my mind, as I did my utmost best to plan out every contingency possible. We were both very frightened, and we held each other as tightly as we could.

This was the first night that we were able to spend together after our wedding, and it could well be our last. It was the longest night that we had to endure.

* * *

23 May 1949

Victory Hotel, Hong Kong

It's been four days since we fled Shanghai. Hong Kong has been one big question mark. We didn't know where to go or what to do next. Everything was expensive. In the end, we settled for a budget hotel named, Victory Hotel. But even the hotel was very costly. With the savings in my possession, we could only stay for about a month or two before going broke.

I thought it was rather ironic to stay at the Victory Hotel. Our feelings were far from victorious. We felt so defeated after having fled the comfort of our homes in Shanghai, with absolutely no idea what we ought to do with our lives.

We felt very lost, and we spent much of our day in the hotel room trying to figure out our next course of action. We had the radio turned on the entire time, in the hopes that good music could lift our moods to inspire us. Instead, we heard the news that Shanghai had just fallen to the Communist.

I could not believe what I heard. I lost myself in a moment of disbelief. Any further delay in leaving Shanghai and we might not have been detained. In fact, I was sure that I would have been tortured. Throughout my time in Shanghai, I proudly wore my KMT uniform everywhere I went. This made me a prime target for the many secret Communist agents lurking in town, especially my ex-lover, Sook Fun. They would have used this moment of victory over Shanghai to exact their vengeance on everyone who supported the KMT.

What a close shave! What luck! I felt as if Divine Providence had directed the planning of our escape so that I could live. But what do I do with this new lease of life? I could not find an answer. I was at a loss for words as I was just so grateful to have narrowly escaped capture.

While Gus and I were very grateful to have escaped in time, our relief slowly transformed into worry. Gus remembered her parents who were reluctant to leave Shanghai, and started worrying about them. Were they now in any danger?

I grabbed hold of Gus and assured her that everything would be alright. We would do our best to establish communication with them as soon as possible. And we would do what we can to help them leave for Hong Kong.

* * *

Eventually, we found an affordable place at Granville Road in Tsim Sha Tsui. It was a little space on the roof of an apartment building. It was the only option I could afford. Thankfully, I was able to build three rooms to accommodate us comfortably. We named our little place "Seventh Heaven," and we were very happy to reside in this little place of refuge.

Before long, Gus' family managed to leave Shanghai and joined us in our little abode. It was a tight squeeze as we now had to accommodate her parents, brother, and two sisters. In our little "Seventh Heaven," we found that life was not only liveable, but even joyous. We could live safely together.

Finances were tight for us, and it was difficult to make ends meet. It was a real struggle. For me, I had to shoulder the additional burden that I may never fly again. Flying had been a huge part of my life. I was heartbroken just thinking about how the disruptions of war had put an end to my studies, and now it seemed to have put an end to my aviation career. I struggled coming to terms with this new reality.

But perhaps it was a good thing that I hadn't come to terms with it. About two or three months later, my old company, the CATC found a way to contact me. As it turned out, I was not the only one to have fled Shanghai. The CATC had moved their operations out of Shanghai to Hong Kong as well. They knew that I had evacuated safety to Hong Kong, and they wanted me to resume my flying duties with them.

The CATC still had much flying to do. Parts of Southern China, such as Guangxi, Sichuan, and Yunnan, were still controlled by various KMT warlords.

The show must go on!

Chapter 19

A REVOLUTIONARY CHANGE

On 1 October 1949, Mao Zedong declared to the world that China was under Communist rule, and was henceforth to be called, the People's Republic of China. It was a crushing defeat for Chiang Kai-shek and the KMT.

I was sorely disappointed, but unsurprised. I had seen this coming for a while. The KMT had been corrupt, and the people were suffering in misery. We fought hard for our freedom, for the KMT only to abuse that freedom to exploit our own kin. It's no wonder people got frustrated and wanted a change in government.

After the Communist takeover, the operations of both Chinese airlines were suspended. All the aircraft 81 in total, belonging to the Central Air Transport Corporation (CATC) and the China National Aviation Corporation (CNAC) were grounded at the Kai Tak International Airport in Hong Kong. Everything was at a standstill, and the staff were divided about what to do next. Meanwhile, we were still considered employees of the CATC, and continued receiving our monthly salary. But it was very frustrating idling around for weeks without work, waiting for further instructions from Management of CATC.

Meanwhile, Zhou Enlai, the Premiere of the People's Republic of China began talks with the Chinese management of the two Chinese airlines. Using *Qiyi* (起義), or "Righteous Uprising," which was the campaign that led to the Communists' successful takeover of China, Premiere Zhou persuaded the management that the future rested in China with the Communists, and not with the KMT in Taiwan. To sweeten the deal, he assured them that the Communist Government would let the airlines continue operations in the same way as before. All employees would receive the exact same pay and benefits as they did previously. And if anyone felt unhappy working in the People's Republic, they were free to leave China at anytime.

This offer seemed like a really good deal. Many CATC and CNAC pilots believed they could continue their flying careers, enjoy the same pay, and maintain the same good quality of life. They were more than willing to fly for the Peoples' Republic of China, and they were excitedly ready to do so at a moment's notice. Premiere Zhou had won them over with his deal.

However, there was one problem: the pilots had no planes to fly. Most of the aircraft belonging to the CATC and CNAC were grounded in Hong Kong due to a pending legal issue. Several parties were contesting ownership of aircraft. The CATC and CNAC were jointly owned by the Americans and the Chinese. The Chinese management of the airlines wanted to claim the aircraft for the Peoples' Republic. On the other hand, the American management of the airlines wanted absolutely nothing to do with the Communists. They adamantly refused to give way to their Chinese counterparts. To further complicate the already messy situation, the British tried to claim ownership as well, arguing that the aircraft were theirs since they were abandoned in Hong Kong (a British territory at that time. A legal battle ensued between these parties to determine the rightful ownership of the aircraft.

The Chinese management were unfazed by the on-going legal tussle, and they were determined to make a very public display of their *Qiyi* against their American counterparts, a symbolic gesture of their commitment to the Peoples' Republic.

On 9 November 1949, the Chinese management of the two airlines made the decision to fly twelve aircraft out of Hong Kong to China. The flights were unauthorised and upset the KMT Government in Taiwan. In response, the KMT sent fighter planes in pursuit of the hijacked aircraft. However, luck was not on the KMT's side, as weather conditions provided heavy cloud cover, shielding the twelve aircraft from the pursuing KMT fighters. Eleven aircraft landed safely in the city of Tianjin. The twelfth aircraft, carrying the management of the CATC and CNAC, landed in the capital of Beijing, where they were greeted by officials from the Communist Party.

The *Qiyi* was a success. The defected managers issued a call to their employees in the Hong Kong head office, and the regional offices to join them in China. Already won over by Premiere Zhou's sweet deal, a total of 2000 employees and their families answered the call and defected into the Peoples' Republic. Some pilots were so inspired by their managers' brave act of defiance, that they took aircraft belonging to the CATC and CNAC and flew them into the Peoples' Republic.

This dealt a huge blow to the American bosses of the CATC and CNAC. Though the Americans won the legal battle for the ownership of the grounded aircraft in Hong Kong, they suffered such a massive loss of staff and aircraft that they were too crippled to continue operations. In the end, they sold off the remaining aircraft to another American airline, much to the fury of the Communists.

* * *

November 1949

With the resounding success of the *Qiyi*, the CATC had moved its operations out of Hong Kong and into Guangzhou, China. This meant that I too had to move as well. I was reluctant to do so as my wife wanted to remain in Hong Kong. I rented a room in Guangzhou just to satisfy my employer's request to move. It was exhausting as I had to shuttle up and down between the two cities. But at least this way, the CATC would not force me to relocate permanently.

While I was in Guangzhou, the Communists wanted us pilots to know more about them and their ideology. They warmly invited us to attend their introductory classes. They told us that we were free to decide whether or not to embrace their ideology. Seeing how friendly they were with their invitation, I thought it was a good opportunity to know more about the Peoples' Liberation Army and their way of thinking.

On the first day, I entered a room and I recognised the familiar faces of my fellow colleagues from the CATC. We were joined by some of the top cadres from the Peoples' Liberation Army, proudly dressed in their uniforms (though their military ranks were obscured). They were very intellectual people and highly sophisticated in the art of speaking.

Over the course of three months, they taught us about how human beings came to be, how we succeeded as a species, and the Communist philosophy. It was all very new and interesting to me as their analysis seemed to be based on facts.

At the end of each lecture, they invited the attendees to write short essays as they wanted to assess our responses toward Communism. In particular, they wanted to know whether we subscribed to it or not. The cadres seemed very earnest in wanting to know us better.

After submitting our essays, the cadres began analysing them in our midst. They began pointing out how certain aspects of our lives were not true, and they required us to revise and rewrite our biographies. One of them came up to me and asked, "It says here that you fought in the war, and then joined the CATC. Do you think what you did was right?"

Proudly I responded, "Yes, it was right, and I am very proud of what I had done."

Little did I know that this invited the attention of more cadres who began questioning the morality of what I had done. "It wasn't right at all," they concluded. They rejected my biography on the grounds that the facts I presented were false. I had to write a new one.

Each time I wrote and submitted another essay, I was subject to more questions: Are you sure that was what you did? Do you think it was right? Why would you believe that when the facts said otherwise?

They were so persuasive, I became very unsure about myself. I was confused. Was everything I did all wrong? Were my beliefs wrong? Could I be certain about anything? I was just so confused. My colleagues in the room did not fare any better either. They were just as confused.

Again and again, I was blasted with an endless barrage of questions. I was less and less certain of myself and what I have done in my life. There were times where I had become so tired, I just wanted to go back home to rest, but I was not allowed to leave the room.

I endured this process of endless questioning for three whole months. It brought me so much anguish and confusion. Though they had succeeded in making me so unsure about myself, there was one thing that I was certain of: I was proud of fighting for the freedom of China as a pilot. That was the one thing they could not change in me, and it was the only anchor that kept me sane.

* * *

War in Korea had broken out. And the Communists in the North had taken over much of the South. This event changed the entire political and military situation. The Americans were worried that the fall of Korea (and eventually Taiwan) would effectively increase the size of the Communist Bloc. President Harry Truman sent troops to assist the Koreans, and a naval fleet to the Straits of Taiwan to end any possibility of a successful Communist invasion.

In response, the Communist Government of China closed the entire coastal region, and moved all airline operations in Guangzhou to the faraway provinces of Ningxia and Inner Mongolia further up north.

There were mixed reactions from many of my colleagues. Some were optimistic about staying, others wanted to leave. Several of my colleagues had no choice but to relocate with the airline. They had fallen in love with the beautiful ladies in the cabin crew, got married, and were yoked to China.

I too, was in a dilemma. If I moved up to the north and later changed my mind, it would be almost impossible to get out of China. The indoctrination session months earlier had unsettled me, and I had long committed to the idea of leaving the CATC. But I could not leave any time I wanted. I had a family to support back in Hong Kong. For weeks I pondered and assessed the situation, waiting for the earliest opportunity, to make a decision.

Perhaps this was the right time to leave.

* * *

July 1950

Guangzhou

This morning was different from all other mornings. The warm glow of the summer sun could not console me. Each step I made towards the CATC office was slow and heavy. Deep within me, I was nursing a heavy heart. So many thoughts raced through my mind. I was tired and felt so lost with myself. I could not concentrate, I could not shut the thoughts of out my head.

I was not born and raised here, yet I considered China my motherland. She had warmly embraced me all these years, gave me a place of refuge, the dignity of a citizen, and most of all, she gave me the wings to fly. More than just grateful, I had a strong love for her, and a deep sense of patriotism. I gave my best to fight for her freedom. I gave all my time and energy to rehabilitate her. Yet, in spite of all these, I had to confront the inevitable dread that one day I had to leave my beloved land.

In the days before, I had discussed the matter at length with my dear wife, Gus. She was expecting and she was due in the weeks to come. It was not an easy decision. We spent days and nights talking about it. And in the end, we decided that for the safety of our family I should leave the CATC and return to Hong Kong. It was time to go.

After what felt like an eternity of walking, I finally made it to the CATC office. And I tended my resignation. Perhaps this might be the end of my flying career.

I left the building heart-broken.

Chapter 20

TO GREENER PASTURES

18 August 1950

David Gregg Hospital for Women and Children, Guangzhou, China

As we were packing our bags for our return to Hong Kong, Gus started going into labour, much earlier than we had expected. We rushed as quickly as we could to the nearest hospital.

At the hospital, the nurses promptly wheeled her into the birthing room. I wanted to beside Gus during this critical moment, but instead, the nurses barred me from entry. "Husbands have to wait outside," said one nurse as she ushered me to a waiting room.

There in the waiting room were several empty chairs, and a few husbands who, like me, were pacing about, anxiously waiting for the delivery of their new-born baby.

It was agonising being made to wait in a separate room. I could not stand beside Gus, I could not comfort her through the rigours of childbirth. A barrage of negative thoughts flooded my mind. What if something bad were to happen to her? What if there was a complication in the childbirth? What if...

After what felt like eternity, a nurse came up to me, saying, "Congratulations! You have a healthy baby boy."

I was delighted to hear those words. Gus was alright, the baby was alright.

The nurse ushered me to the ward where Gus laid, now exhausted from using all her might to deliver the baby. Cusped in her arms was a tiny little baby boy, wrapped in a white towel. The baby was asleep, probably tired from the excitement of entering into this new world. His face looked so calm and serene, and his presence filled both Gus and I with a great sense of peace and joy.

In some ways, this baby reminded me of my close buddy, Fred Gurwitz, who manned the Directional Finder during the Second World War back in Hanzhong. He too was a very calm and gentle person. It was rare to meet someone who could fill you with a sense of peace amidst the anxieties of war. I thought it was also very apt for Fred Gurwitz to be named as such, since the name, "Frederick," means "peaceful ruler."

Here was a little baby born in a time of turmoil and uncertainty, born in a time where peace seemed impossible. Here was our little baby boy calmly asleep, unbothered by the conflicts of this world, as if certain that peace will prevail. Here was our little one, our beacon of hope that everything in this turbulent world would soon be alright.

It was for this reason that we named our first-born son Frederick.

I held baby Fred in my arms for the first time. I was overwhelmed with joy. Here in my arms was my flesh and blood, the fruit of my love, my pride and joy.

I was now a father. Everything will be alright.

*** * * ***

June 1951

Hong Kong

Life in Hong Kong was tough. At first, I worried about what we could do to support the family. But Gus was very confident in our abilities. She assured me that our educational background and our ability to communicate in English were sure guarantees of employment. And true enough, within a few weeks, we found employment. Gus worked in an accounting firm, while I worked in a trading company. We struggled hard to make ends meet. And though our finances were strained, we managed to earned enough to feed everyone under our roof.

Personally, my greatest struggle was having to shoulder the burden that I may never be able to fly again. Flying had been a huge part of my life. I was heartbroken just thinking about how an unfortunate series of events had radically changed my life. First, it was the Japanese invasion that put an end to my studies, and now the uncertainties of a Communist regime have clipped my wings in what seemed to be the end of my aviation career.

It was difficult for me to come to terms with this new reality. While I was relatively content with my life in Hong Kong, the urge to fly again was constantly pulsing through my veins.

One fine day, I received a letter from two very old buddies of mine, M. S. Leong and Johnny Tai. They once flew for the Chinese National

Aviation Corporation (CNAC), but left China shortly before me as they were worried about the heightening tensions in and around China.

Both of them found a fresh opportunity in the tropical island of Singapore, where a certain airline was rapidly expanding and was in urgent need of pilots. The airline was called, Malayan Airways, and it was started in 1947 by the British company, Mansfield & Co. Limited. For years, the Airline comprised solely of expatriate pilots from Australia and the United Kingdom. But as the business expanded, the Airline began making significant changes and expanded its fleet to incorporate six DC-3 aircraft. For the very first time in the Airline's history, Malayan Airways was looking to hire local Malayan pilots.

M. S. and Johnny learnt that I had left the China Air Transport Corporation (CATC) and urged me to join them in Malaya. They also urged Y. W. Fong, another very close buddy of ours to do the same. He too had left the CNAC recently out of fear that he could not leave China if anything happened.

"Come join us in Singapore! It will be like the good old times in Shanghai."

* * *

I have known M. S. Leong since we were young. We lived in the same neighbourhood and we grew up playing soccer together back in Ipoh, Malaya. We were very close friends. So close that people loved to call us, "The Twins."

M. S.'s full name was Ming Sen, which translates to "bright star." I thought his parents had given him a very apt name, as he shone very brightly in primary and secondary school, excelling in both sports and studies. He was very athletic and was top in every sport he competed in. He was so good, no one ever came close to his records. He had a table full of trophies in his house.

M. S. did incredibly well in his studies, and aced the Cambridge leaving examinations. But as we came from a small town, there were not many opportunities available. He went on to study commercial typing and shorthand. At that time, I had just returned from Hong Kong, having attempted to matriculate at Hong Kong University, and I saw the boundless opportunities that awaited us. And so I persuaded his parents that he should study in Hong Kong with me. There, he would have a much brighter future.

His parents agreed to send both him and his brother, Swee Seng. His mother made me promise to take good care of them. I gave her my promise and assured her that I would not let her down. When the Japanese invaded Hong Kong, I stayed true to my word and made it my personal responsibility to ensure the two brothers made it safely to China.

After that, I did not get a chance to see M. S. again until September 1944 in Kunming. This happened when I was on my way back to China after my "Miracle Year" training in America. It had been three years since I ensured his safe passage out of Hong Kong. It was an emotional meeting of old friends. But that meeting was rudely interrupted when Japanese bombers suddenly attacked Kunming, dropping bombs over our heads. We ran to the nearby caves for shelter. We survived that night of bombings, and we both laughed and cried together. It was just so ironic that we left under perilous circumstances, and met once again under a similarly perilous situation.

We were both delighted to learn that we had become pilots. As kids, none of us had aspired to be pilots. The thought was so remote it never once crossed our minds. And so it was just incredible how the Second World War brought about a twist and turn of events that led to us becoming pilots. I was a pilot with the Chinese Air Force, while he was a commercial pilot for the CNAC.

Our destinies must have been intertwined as we met each other on countless occasions ever since then.

* * *

I got to know Johnny Tai, and Y. W. Fong after I joined the CATC. The four of us were based in Shanghai, and together, we rented a house in the posh district of the French Concession. We were like close brothers. Perhaps this was because we shared a common heritage and a common homeland despite working and living in a far distant land. We spent a lot of our time sharing about our day and the people we encountered, and we often reminisced our childhood days in Malaya.

As young bachelors, we organised many parties in our house and attended just as many parties and events. We were regularly up to some mischief. We had a lot of fun together.

One time, the four of us crashed a party and got kicked out almost immediately. The organiser was a pilot from the CNAC named, Herbert. He was interested in a lady by the name of Diana, and he threw a party to impress her. Diana was actually a friend of mine, and I had promised her days ago that I would find her a boyfriend. Not wanting to break my promise to Diana, I decided to match Y. W. with her on the day of the party. Before we crashed the party, I grabbed hold of Y. W., looked him in the eyes, and said, "I have found a girlfriend for you." Y. W. was very excited. At the party, I found Diana and introduced Y. W. to her. There and then, they fell in love and kissed each other (they eventually became happily married). Herbert was shocked by what had happened in front of him and he kicked all of us out of his house. It was an evening to remember!

* * *

The thought of working with my close buddies in the same airline excited me greatly, though I felt that it was all very ironic for me. In the first place, I left Malaya and travelled thousands of miles north in search for security and a better future. I did not expect to return to Malaya ever again. Yet, here I was, making a return back to where it all started for the exact same reason of having a better future. Nonetheless, I was overjoyed to have the opportunity to resume my flying career once more.

As I began planning for my return to Malaya, I realised that my Chinese passport was no longer valid. And unfortunately, I had severed my connections with China: I was no longer fighting for the KMT, and I stopped flying for the CATC. The governments of Taiwan and China would not issue me a new passport. I had lost my status as a citizen.

The only option left for me was to apply for a new passport with the Malayan Embassy in Hong Kong. Upon receiving my new passport, I felt a deep sense of frustration and disappointment. Once again, I was a "British protected person of the Federated Malay States," as it was stated on my passport. I was no longer a citizen of any land, just a mere person "protected" by my colonial masters. It was disappointing. I had a hard time accepting that status.

But I had to endure it for the sake of seeking greener pastures for my family. I held on to the hope that everything would be alright in time to come.

* * *

August 1951

Singapore

After a slow boat ride, Y. W. Fong and I arrived in Singapore, a British crown south of Malaya, at the tip of the Malay Peninsula. Managing Director of Malayan Airways, Captain Roger Mollard, interviewed us, and he was impressed by our extensive flying records. Without any hesitation, he immediately accepted us as pilots for the Airline.

And just like that, M.S. Leong, Johnny Tai, Y.W. Fong, and I became the first four local pilots to join Malayan Airways. It was a proud moment for us to be the pioneer batch of Malayans in an all-white working environment.

But behind the prestige and honour of being the first locals to join the Airline, was a dark side of the hardship and struggles that we had to endure since our first day as pilots. As locals, as subjects of our colonial masters, we were looked down upon by many expatriate pilots. They regarded our so-called "Chinese" training as somehow vastly inferior to their "Western" flight training.

The four of us had about five years of flying experience in China (clocking a total of about 3000 flying hours each). This meant that we were just as experienced as some of the more senior pilots in the Airline. Yet, the Airline disregarded all our years of valuable experience, including our flying experience during the Second World War. Instead, they gave us a low rank of First Officer. It was awfully humiliating, especially for M. S. Leong and Johnny Tai, as they previously held the esteemed rank of Captain at CNAC.

We were painfully aware of the racism in the organisation and the discrimination towards us. Some of the expatriate pilots did not hesitate in expressing their prejudices openly. The junior expatriate officers often overlooked our rank as First Officers, and they often overrode our decisions even though we were more experienced in the air than they were. And they could disobey us with no disciplinary consequences whatsoever. It was infuriating and quite humiliating.

It's not like we could leave and join another airline if we wanted to. China was no longer an option for us. So if we wanted to continue our flying careers, this was the only place to be. We had no choice but to stay and endure the humiliation.

* * *

As the months went by, Malayan Airways began hiring more locals, and entrusted the training of the new cadets to the hands of a few expatriate instructors. I heard stories of how aggressive these instructors were during training. Some of the cadets were so intimidated by them that they could not perform under pressure and dropped out. Only a few cadets survived the ordeal to become pilots.

This made me very angry. How were we supposed to have more local pilots if the instructors bullied our local cadets? I was more upset by the fact that I could not do anything about it. My words carried little weight in the Airline, and I was not in a position to do anything. I made a promise to myself that I would do something about this when the opportunity ever arose.

* * *

Thankfully, despite the rampant discrimination, there were a handful of expatriate pilots, such as Captain John Osmond and Captain John Muraille, who were quite supportive of us, even to the extent of warmly embracing our local culture. They were some of the most trustworthy colleagues and friends we could rely on. However, there was very little time to socialise with each other as our flight schedules were incredibly hectic.

Each day, as part of our regular flight routine, we had to follow a pattern known as, "round the houses." Each leg lasted as long as 12 hours. Flights originated from Singapore and would head northwards to cover Malacca, Kuala Lumpur, Ipoh, Taiping, and Penang. At Penang, a different set of pilots and cabin crew would board the plane for the next leg, starting from Penang, and head southwards to cover Alor Star, Kota Bharu, Kuala Terengganu and Kuantan, Kuala Lumpur, Malacca, and finally back to Singapore. There was also the East Malaysia destinations like Kuching, Sibu, Labuan, Kota Kinabalu, Sandakan and Brunei.

As the flight patterns were fixed, we were often able to meet for quick lunches at the Penang Flying Club. Lunch in Penang was something we always looked forward to. The food was great too, and it was often one of our highlights of the day. The delicious food was cooked by a Hainanese migrant, who was assisted by his wife and daughter.

Though it only lasted half an hour long, it was a great time for us to catch up with one another. It was through these short lunches where we truly bonded.

* * *

15 January 1952

Kowloon Maternal Hospital, Hong Kong

While I was flying around Singapore and Malaya, Gus stayed behind in Hong Kong to look after her parents and our son. Despite my hectic flight schedule, I always found the time write short letters to her. Each time I thought of her, I would pick up a piece of paper — any piece of paper I could find — and I would pen a message, where I shared with her my thoughts and feelings. I sent many letters each day, and I was certain I must have kept the postmen very busy!

After an uneventful flight, I was finally back in Hong Kong. It had been about half a year since I last saw her. I was eager to meet her. But when I got home to our "Seven Heaven" apartment, I learnt that she was in the hospital. I dropped my bags and rushed over to Kowloon Maternal Hospital.

I felt a sense of déjà vu visiting the hospital. I asked to see my wife, and the nurse told me to wait in the waiting room. Once more, I beheld a familiar sight of a room full of empty chairs and anxious men pacing around. I was a lot calmer than before. By now, I was a seasoned veteran. I knew what I was expecting. I sat down on one of the empty chairs and patiently waited for the news.

And just like I was reliving the moment one and a half years ago, a nurse came up to me, saying, "Congratulations! You have a healthy baby girl."

I followed the nurse to the ward and there was Gus, lying on the bed, her arms cusped around our little baby girl. I held Gus' hand and stood in awe, admiring our beautiful little daughter.

We named her Catherine, after the great Saint Catherine of Labouré, who in spite of the miraculous events that happened in her life, quietly and humbly spent her lifetime tending to the needs of the sick and the poor. We had witnessed the great poverty around us when we were in Shanghai, and now, we too had to struggle financially to make ends meet. We understood how difficult it was for people to thrive in such conditions. It was our hope that baby Catherine would grow up with a heart of compassion and a sincere care for the last, the lost, and the least.

We affectionately called her Lulu, as baby Catherine reminded Gus so much of a doll I gave her. It was my first gift to her when we were still dating and Gus named it Lulu after the main character of the movie, "Lulu Belle," whose strong and rich character in the film impressed her very much.

Gus cherished that doll with all her heart as it was a symbol of my love. She took good care of Lulu as it was her way of showing me how much she treasured our relationship. And now, we have our precious daughter, the fruit of our love, the gift we gave to each other. Catherine wasn't just Gus' Lulu, she was our Lulu, whom we could cherish and nurture lovingly together.

* * *

April 1953

53 Pulasan Road, Singapore

More than a year had passed and I finally found a house at 53 Pulasan Road. It was conducive for Gus and I to raise Fred and Lulu. It took us a while for the entire family to come under one roof. Gus was reluctant to move, partly because she was worried about leaving her parents behind in Hong Kong, and partly because she was apprehensive that she could not cope with the tropical heat.

After much coaxing, she took the plunge and brought the kids over to Singapore. The first couple of months were torturous to Gus. She developed skin problems due to the heat and the humidity. It was a painful ordeal for her, and it was difficult for her to raise two kids while struggling with the skin problem.

Thankfully, as the months went by, her body acclimated to the humidity and she eventually fell in love living life on this tropical island.

I was overjoyed to finally have my family with me. With them around, Singapore was starting to feel a lot like home.

* * *

May 1954

Over the years, M. S. Leong, Johnny Tai, Y. W. Fong, and I, had been putting up with the discriminations. We thought quite optimistically that we could win their confidence through our professional abilities at work. Perhaps we could impress the expatriate pilots and the Airline would come to recognise our flying background and respect us for who we were. Yet, month after month went by and we saw no improvement. We were always inferior by virtue of our skin colour.

Eventually, M. S. Leong and Johnny Tai got tired of waiting. And eventually, they called it quits.

Since their experience and seniority were never once recognised, they decided they would find an airline that would. In their quest for greener pastures, they joined an airline called, Nanyang Airways. It was not a very well-known airline as it specialised in delivering newspapers printed in Singapore to towns all over Malaya. At the very least, the Airline recognised their seniority and experienced. They flew as Captains and received a much higher salary.

M. S. Leong persuaded me to join him in Nanyang Airways, but I was reluctant. Sure, I was unhappy with all the discrimination, but I hadn't yet reached a point where I was fed up with Malayan Airways.

Eventually, I discovered that my expatriate counterparts of the same level were earning $200 more than me each month (an incredibly huge sum of money at that time). There was nothing that could justify the enormous wage gap. I was far more experienced than they were, and we were doing the exact same job. The only difference was the colour of my skin.

I objected to this huge disparity in the pay, but my concerns were treated like it was a trivial matter and the management nonchalantly brushed the matter aside. It was this lack of respect that was the last straw that broke the camel's back.

Enough was enough. I tended my resignation and left to join my friends in Nanyang Airways.

Chapter 21

EMBRACING NEW IDENTITIES

19 July 1954

Singapore

Over at Nanyang Airways, I enjoyed a much better pay and flew with the prestigious rank of a Captain. Life as a pilot was very good, and after such a long time, Gus and I finally did not have to worry about our finances for the family.

But perhaps this was too good to be true. Slightly after a month, Nanyang Airways was forced to close down. The newspaper companies had found a more affordable mode of delivery by land, and they had no need for the Airline. Overnight, we were all suddenly unemployed.

I knew Malayan Airways still had a severe shortage of pilots, and they urgently needed experienced pilots like myself. There might be a chance that they were willing to take me back. But since I had resigned in a fit of anger at the blatant discrimination against local pilots, I figured they might not want me back.

I had to eat humble pie. I tried my luck contacting the Managing Director.

He was quite surprised to hear from me so soon. And to my surprise, he was quite happy to take me back with open arms, and he offered me a salary that was equal to that of the expatriate pilots. We were both very pleased with the arrangement. I was back with Malayan Airways.

* * *

It's amazing how fast children grow. In what felt like a blink of an eye, Fred and Catherine were not little babies anymore. They could walk and they could talk. And this meant that I had so much more to do as a father.

This realisation made me question what sort of father I myself wanted to be. And I started to think about the way my parents raised me.

My father was a stern and demanding man who challenged us to rise above our limits to be more than what we were. He was affectionate yet firm in inculcating us with the right values. It was essential to him that every member of the family (including his employees whom he treated as his extended family) felt a strong sense of belonging. He believed and showed us by way of example that this was achieved through a strong familial culture that emphasised the importance of family ties.

My mother was always so full of love and compassion. She was the heart of the household. Whenever we misbehaved, she would always plead to our father to be forgiving and lenient with us so that he would not cane us. She taught us by her example to always be merciful and forgiving, to let go of past mistakes, and to embrace each other despite the error of our ways. In her eyes, no one was ever so bad as to be denied love and care.

These were the qualities my parents exhibited that shaped me into the person I have come to be. Having seen them demonstrate these qualities by their own example, I thought it might be ideal that I should emulate these qualities in my own way as a father to my own children.

One of the first things I did in my quest to build a strong family culture was to organise weekly family outings to the Chinese Swimming Club in Amber Road. Gus and I brought them into the baby pool and we taught them how to be confident in the water. I would hold their hands as I taught them to do the basic strokes. As they got more and more confident, I brought them out to the deeper parts of the pool. Once they could swim confidently on their own, I introduced Fred and Catherine to competitive swimming so that I could imbue them with the values of good sportsmanship.

It was a lot of fun and I believed such activities helped greatly with family bonding.

* * *

When Fred was still a young child, he came home one day from school complaining that he could not see so well. Gus and I took him to an optician in North Bridge Road. The optician found that Fred's eyesight had deteriorated due to myopia and he needed a pair of glasses.

The news left little Fred devastated.

Fred looked up to me a lot. He wanted to emulate me in every way that he could. His biggest ambition was to become a pilot, just like me. Naturally, I felt so proud of him. To fuel his interest in aviation, I bought him plastic model aeroplanes that he could build and play.

He was so sure that he would become a pilot. But with news of his poor eyesight, Fred knew that he could no longer fulfil his dreams of becoming a pilot.

He cried long and hard that day. Gus and I were at a loss for words.

After dinner, I sat at my desk contemplating what exactly I could do or say to console Fred. I thought about the kind words my father and mother might have said in a situation like this, and I remembered how my parents were standing by my side as an advisor, giving me their inputs in a very soft and encouraging way. Their approach helped me a lot, and I thought I should do likewise.

That night, I wrote a letter to Fred, consoling him that there were many other opportunities out there in the world. I shared about how my dreams were dashed by so many circumstances beyond my control, and in spite of all that, I was still blessed as a pilot with a beautiful family. I encouraged him to explore other areas of interest, and I told him that I would always be so proud of him regardless of the path in life he chose.

As the months went by, Fred came to terms that he could not be a pilot. I began buying him a variety of toys to stimulate his mind and help him discover other areas that he might have an interest in. I believed that was what my parents would have done, and that was the least I could do as a father.

***

November 1957

St. Patrick's School, Singapore

Under the leadership of Chief Minister Lim Yew Hock, Singapore underwent major constitutional changes. After much negotiations, the British Government finally agreed to grant complete internal self-government to Singapore. No longer was the island a mere colony, but an autonomous self-ruling state, with its own citizenry.

The Government of Singapore began setting up citizen registration points all over the island. And on 15 October 1957, Chief Minister Lim announced how easy it was to register as a citizen: "You go through one door, come out another door, and you are a Singapore citizen."

Registering myself and my family as citizens was a big step. The question of my identity and belonging was suddenly thrust upon me. I felt very much at home in Singapore. The culture, the climate, the food, and the language were all very familiar to me, just like in the days of my youth growing up in Ipoh.

But what exactly did it mean to be a "citizen" of Singapore? It was such a new and alien concept for so many of us. Would this mean having to abandon my Chinese identity or my Chinese heritage? What about my ties to China?

I could not find an answer. No one around me really understood the full implications of being a citizen, yet many people across the island were eager to register. Some assumed that it was just mere paperwork and life would go on normally as if this never happened. Others imagined a new culture, a new identity. Some others were just like me, frank to admit that we had no idea what awaited us after registration.

For me, the impetus to register was driven largely by practical concerns. On our most recent holiday vacation to the United States, we were stopped at the immigration checkpoint and interrogated. Everyone in my family was born in a different region, and so we each held different passports. I was born in Ipoh, my wife was born in Shanghai, Fred was born in Guangzhou, and Catherine was born in Hong Kong. The customs officer feared that we might have been engaged in child trafficking. It was a nuisance wasting hours of our precious vacation time trying to explain and prove that we were all one family. If we could all bear the same Singapore passport, family vacations would go much smoother in the future.

But I did have one other motivation for embracing citizenship. Up till now, as someone coming from Ipoh, I was still holding a British passport indicating that I was a "British protected person." This meant that I had to carry with me all the restrictions and limitations that came with being a second-class citizen, while surrounded by many others who did not have this issue (people born in Singapore did not have this second-class status). I hated having to carry such a denigratory status. Embracing citizenship meant that I could be freed from that lowly status.

The day finally came for my family and I to register. We walked over to the nearest registration centre situated in the compound of St. Patrick's School. There was a long queue. But after an hour of waiting, our turn had arrived.

All we had to do was to fill in an application form, stand before a civil servant, and raise our right hands as we swore an oath. In less than a minute, we were done. It was surprisingly simple, and I was glad that I had gone through the process.

I had a new identity. I was no longer a second-class citizen, or some inferior person by virtue of my race or skin colour. I was finally an actual citizen, recognised as having an equal standing with any other citizen around the world. There was a moment of quiet jubilation in me, knowing that those days are now over.

On the appointed day, Lee visited the Malayan Airways company to speak to our Managing Director. We were all present for that meeting, all fifteen of us local pilots. What was truly remarkable about it was that before Lee could sit down on his chair, the Managing Director agreed to the terms of our request. In an instant, we got a pay increase that put every local pilot's salary on par with our expatriate contemporaries.

From that day forth, the expatriates learnt about our strength and stopped bullying us. They knew they had to be careful, especially since we had the support of Lee Kuan Yew.

* * *

In the months that followed, we began to notice a considerable change within the organisation. But this did not mean that the discriminations stopped immediately. Discrimination still persisted but in more subtle ways.

The management of Malayan Airways began identifying local pilots as potential candidates to become the first local commander of the Airline. At first, M. S. Leong, Johnny Tai, Y. W. Fong and I — the pioneer batch of local pilots — were excited by the news. But we soon learnt that we were disqualified from consideration. They did not reveal the reason, but it soon became clear that only local pilots trained by the expatriate instructors qualified as candidates.

Naturally, the four of us were quite upset by this. Our "Chinese" flight training was considered inferior. But in the end, we chose not to fight this battle since we were already quite pleased to know that one of our own locals would become the first captain. This in itself was already good enough for us.

* * *

One of our local pilots, Charlie Chan, was promoted to the rank of Captain, making him the first local commander in the Airline. He was immensely grateful for my efforts in pushing for change in the Airline. And he requested me to be his co-pilot on his maiden flight as Captain.

I was honoured by his invitation. This meant that it was the first time that we could fly with an all-local crew! At long last, the Airline had removed the discriminatory policy that local pilots had to be supervised by an expatriate.

This was a huge milestone in Malaya's aviation history. The local pilots were now recognised as equals with the expatriate pilots. This gave us local pilots a bright hope for the future.

The sky's the limit for what we locals can now achieve.

Chapter 22

PAVING THE WAY WITH HARDSHIP

By the early 1960s, air travel became more affordable and it was a privilege no longer confined to the rich and famous. More people wanted to fly and travel the world for business and for leisure. This led to a tremendous increase in the demand for air travel. To cater to the increased demand in the region, Malayan Airways began expanding its routes beyond the Malay Peninsula to places like Jakarta, Palembang, and Medan in Indonesia, Saigon in Vietnam, and Rangoon in Burma.

However, the expansion was too rapid, and the management had planned very ambitious flight itineraries. With only six DC-3 aircraft and a shortage of pilots, we had no choice but to clock about 70–80 flying hours each week. The hours were long and arduous. But one good thing that came out of it was that we grew very close to one another. More than just colleagues, we became very close friends because of the many hours we spent together up in the air. Even on the ground, we travelled together, ate together, and even went shopping together. Over time, we grew to become a very close knit community of pilots and cabin crew.

We were painfully aware that the ambitious itineraries were not sustainable in the long-term. With such packed schedules, pilots would eventually become fatigued, posing a huge risk to flight safety. Malayan Airways recruited more pilots, but even that was still not enough to make up for the shortfall. But there were not many trained pilots available for hire, so the Airline had to seek talent elsewhere.

It was at this time that the Commonwealth Nations started the Colombo Plan, a scholarship to train the best and brightest students from Southeast Asia so that they could return as qualified professionals to support the economic and social development of their respective country. Not having the funds or the means to train new pilots, Malayan Airways made use of this timely opportunity, and sent five local cadet pilots for flight training in Bangalore.

Seeing the success of the Colombo Plan, the Airline managed to put together an Air Service Training Scholarship the following year to send cadet pilots to Scotland for flight training. It was such a lucrative scholarship that the Airline was able to attract ten of the brightest students in Malaya and Singapore over the next two years.

* * *

4 October 1961

Bayan Lepas Airport, Penang, Malaya

This day started off very much like a routine day of flying. I had just finished catching up with some of my fellow pilots over our usual lunch gathering at the Penang Flying Club, and proceeded to board the DC-3 aircraft, in preparation for take-off. In all, we had ten passengers on board, including one infant.

The aircraft took off from the runway. Everything seemed to be going well, but I had a nagging feeling that something was not right. Half an hour later, the aircrew and I could feel the entire aircraft vibrating very strongly. This was unlike the vibrations one typically encounters during take-off or during turbulence.

Unsure as to what was happening, I checked the gauges on the dashboard. To my surprise, the gauge indicated that the temperature of the aircraft was rising while the oil pressure was dropping. This felt like a very familiar experience. It reminded me of the time my aircraft was shot while we were out on a bombing mission during the Second World War. And it became clear to me what was going on.

One of the engines was on fire.

I had only one working engine left to use. There and then, I had to make a split-second judgement call as Captain of the aircraft. I had been promoted to a Captain about three months ago, and it felt surreal having to exercise an emergency judgement call for the first time. Lives were at stake. I needed to act quickly.

I made the decision to turn the plane around and return to the airport in Penang. By my estimates, we had enough altitude to glide the aircraft and land safely on the runway. I radioed the control tower of Bayan Lepas Airport, informing them of what was happening. The control tower responded that they had cleared the runway and they were ready to receive our aircraft.

The vibrations made it somewhat difficult for me to manoeuvre the aircraft. Thankfully, this was not an unfamiliar encounter. Sitting in the cockpit, I felt like I was returning from a bombing mission during the war in China, where my aircraft was badly damaged by the enemy's guns.

I was still in control. I knew exactly what to do.

I instructed the cabin crew to carry out all that was necessary in preparation for a crash landing. This was just a standard safety protocol for the worst possible scenario. But I was confident that we would not crash, and I assured the crew that everything was under control.

About half an hour later, my aircraft drew close to the airport. As we glided down in our descent, I lowered the landing gears of the aircraft. The hard part was trying to land the aircraft safety. It was difficult to angle the plane for landing with only one engine. But I knew what I had to do. My missions in the war were all rehearsals for this moment now.

In that crucial moment, the aircraft touched down onto the runway. It was a rough and bumpy landing. I applied the brakes and the aircraft came to a halt. We had landed safe and sound. There were no injuries.

I averted a crash that day.

* * *

29 January 1962

Mount Alvernia Hospital, Singapore

Gus and I were back in the hospital again to deliver our third child. We were very excited to welcome a new member to our family.

The hospital was run by the Franciscan Missionaries of the Divine Motherhood. They were a group of Catholic sisters who were trained in medicine and nursing. When Gus entered into labour, the sisters promptly wheeled her into the delivery room. I waited outside the room. I felt slightly worried that complications might arise during labour, but at the same time, I thought to myself, perhaps I was just being paranoid. The first two pregnancies went smoothly, so this one would turn out fine.

Just as I was entertaining that thought, a loud commotion began stirring within the delivery room. A medical sister ran out of the room. She returned shortly after, accompanied by a few sisters, some carrying bags of blood, others wheeling a trolley full of equipment. This was not a promising sign. I had to know what was happening behind the doors. I stopped one of the sisters and asked. She responded, telling me that some complications had arisen during childbirth. Gus had lost a lot of blood, and they were doing all they could to save her and our baby.

I was overwhelmed with anguish. I did not know what to do. I never felt so helpless before.

* * *

The doctors succeeded in saving the baby. It was a baby boy, but he was so frail and weak that he had to be placed under observation in the Intensive Care Unit (ICU).

When I saw our precious baby, I thought it would be fitting to name him after my Tibetan buddy back in the Chinese Air Force, Kasun Chu Pee. Everyone in the Air Force called him David. He was a big and strong person, and we hoped that little David would one day grow up to be just as big and strong as him. We also hoped that our son would grow up to be a great person and do great things just like King David in the Bible.

More importantly, we gave our precious baby the name, "David," because it means "beloved." We almost lost him before we had him, and this event made us cherish him even more.

* * *

Gus too survived the ordeal. I was informed by the doctors that she almost died that day. She had lost an incredible amount of blood and her heart stopped beating. The doctors had to resuscitate her.

Gus laid in the hospital bed too frail to move. I could not bear to leave her side. When she awoke, she was so delighted to see me. She cried profusely and told me how happy she was to see me again. She could not remember all that had happened during delivery. All she knew was that she was in a lot of pain, and suddenly she found herself in a dark tunnel heading towards a light. But before she reached the light, everything went dark.

She noticed that she had lost vision in one eye. And it distressed her so greatly to lose half her sight.

Gus was a strong lady. She had the will to live, and she struggled and did her best to continue looking after the children despite her condition.

However, life in the family changed forever since then. Gus' health deteriorated slowly with each passing day. She felt tired easily and had a lot of difficulty looking after the children. Eventually, one of her kidneys failed and she had to undergo an operation to remove it.

It was heart-wrenching witnessing all these things happening to Gus. It was painful knowing that there was so little I could do to make her better. All I could do was to I seek out the best medical treatment from around the world. I brought her overseas to Hong Kong, and even to the United Kingdom in the hope of finding a treatment that can help her.

*   *   *

September 1963

On 16 September 1963, the British granted independence to the states of Singapore, Sabah, and Sarawak. These three joined the Federation of Malaya to become Malaysia. To reflect this great change in the geopolitical scene, the Airline was renamed to Malaysian Airways.

Mansfield & Co. Limited, the British company that owned Malayan Airways relinquished management of the company to the Malaysian Government. The British Overseas Aviation Corporation (now known as British Airways) and Qantas Empire Airways, both private shareholders of the Airline, provided the necessary technical assistance.

The Airline continued to expand its destinations, and added new aircraft, like the Viscount and the Fokker Friendship F-27s to its fleet.

Once more, the Airline needed more pilots. Having gained our independence from the British, we wanted very much to groom our own local talent. The Malaysian Government stepped in to provide assistance, and made arrangements for new cadet pilots to be trained in Australia, Indonesia, and the Philippines. Upon completion of their training, these cadets would return to Malaysia to serve a bond as pilots for their national Airline. The scheme attracted a sizeable number of young men who had just completed their studies, and they were sent to various parts of the region to commence their training.

By this time, the first batch of cadet pilots was returning from their flight training in Bangalore under the Colombo Plan. Many more cadets were scheduled to return in the months to come. We also had a small but steady stream of locals who had acquired a private pilot license. They too wanted to become commercial pilots for the Airline. However, the training they received only prepared them for light aircraft. They were unprepared to fly the DC-3 Dakota commercial aeroplanes, which was far larger and heavier than the ones they were familiar with. To fly the DC-3, they needed to undergo a conversion flight training programme, and to pass a series of mandatory tests as required by the Republic of Singapore Department of Civil Aviation.

Malaysian Airways needed more flight instructors to train these cadets. And for the first time in our aviation history, the Airline decided that we needed local flight instructors.

When I heard the news, I remembered the promise I made to myself more than ten years ago. The promise was that when the opportunity arose for me to be an instructor, I would seize it without hesitation and make a difference in the training of our local cadets. Many of the expatriate instructors were still very mean and aggressive to the local cadets, and this made it terribly difficult for these young men to complete and pass their flight training. If we wanted a truly national Airline, we needed more local pilots. I was determined to do my best to resolve this problem.

I stepped forward enthusiastically and volunteered to be a flight instructor. The management was very pleased. They recognised the fact that I was one of the most experienced senior pilots in the Airline, especially with my flying experience. Above all, I stood out for having averted an air crash two years ago by safely landing an aircraft with a failed engine. I was the ideal candidate for the job.

What I lacked, however, were the paper qualifications necessary for the job. As the first local flight instructor, this meant that I had to undergo the required training under the expatriate instructors. This was a minor setback for me. I had to endure and put up with their aggressive and discriminatory antics. It was not easy having to endure insults and humiliation in the cockpit. But I persevered and struggled through it for the sake of locals who were aspiring to be pilots. I had to work very hard to prove myself to these expatriate pilots that I was worthy and qualified to join their ranks.

*　*　*

24 January 1964

After many months of hardship, I succeeded in proving myself to the expatriate instructors and earned the necessary paper qualifications. And on this day, Malaysian Airways appointed me a Training Captain, placing me in charge of leading the Airline's training programme for our local cadets.

I was immensely thrilled, but I knew I could not do this all by myself. So I roped in my closest friend and colleague, M. S. Leong, to help me.

M.S. was initially planning to fly the new Comet aircraft. But when I told him about our mandate to train and develop our own pool of local pilots, he too was excited about it and came on board with me.

We had long tolerated years of discrimination in our homeland, and our generation was deprived of so many opportunities. Now the opportunity was finally in our hands. Now was our chance to make things right and pave the way for a future generation of local pilots for the Airline.

Chapter 23

DADDY-O

April 1964

Paya Lebar Airport, Singapore

After weeks of intense preparation, M. S. Leong and I were ready to receive our first batch of cadets. Four of them were scholars who had just returned from their basic flight training in Bangalore. The other six were new recruits who had previously trained with the local flying club. Now they needed to be trained on the bigger commercial aircraft like the DC-3 that Malaysian Airways operated.

On our first day of training, I was greeted by ten very eager cadets. Though they were very excited, they were anxious as they were well-aware of how much more complicated commercial aircraft were compared to what they had learnt, and the various training exercises were done in mid-air.

I was well-aware just how worried they were and decided to ease them slowly into the training. I brought the cadets, two-by-two at a time, into the DC-3's small cockpit and showed them the various buttons, levers, and switches that they needed to know, in order to fly the aircraft control. I could see it in their faces how overwhelmed they were, struggling to remember the sheer number of things.

This made me realise just how much patience I had to exercise to train these cadets well. And all the more so especially since I wanted all of them to pass the training and become great pilots for the Airline. I was very grateful that I had some practice in being nurturing and patient from just being a father to my children at home. I believed I could exercise the same fatherly type of care to my cadets to help them spread their wings.

Each time I saw them struggle, I paused my teaching and engaged them in some casual conversation. I found that the more comfortable and relaxed they were, the better they were at learning.

Once the cadets were confident in remembering all that I had taught, I had to administer a test to ensure that they were indeed familiar with the aircraft. Once they had passed the test, we could proceed to the next stage of training, known as 'Base Training.'

* * *

As the name suggests, Base Training was done entirely at the 'base,' or in our case, the airport. I taught the basics like how to take off and land on the runway; how to manoeuvre the aircraft and carry out unusual manoeuvres; how to cut the engine; how to make the engine stall; and more importantly how to recover from a stalled engine.

On each flight, I brought cadets, two at a time, on board the DC-3. I would first demonstrate the procedures while they observed what needed to be done. When they were ready, they would take turns to helm the controls. Even though these procedures were already familiar to the cadets, flying a commercial aircraft was a very new experience, vastly different from what they had learnt previously.

Flight training at that time was nothing like the modern flight training of today. There were no flight simulators. And so, training had to be conducted in person in an actual aircraft. If any of them lacked confidence, the risk of an accident was very high.

I thought that my experience training new pilots for the Chinese Air Force had prepared me very well as a flight instructor here. I was wrong, and quite unprepared for what would happen with my first batch of cadets. These cadets did not go through the rigours of military training. They were significantly less stoic and more nervous. Despite all that I had done to familiarise them with the controls of the aircraft, many things did not go according to plan.

Admittedly, the DC-3 was not an easy aircraft to manoeuver. The design of the aircraft was such that the aircraft was always tilting upwards whenever it was on the ground. The cockpit was not level with the ground, and it was very difficult to see what was on the ground in front of us through the window. Moreover, the tailwheel of the DC-3 was fixed to the back of the aircraft, making the act of landing far more dangerous than it should be. If the pilot failed to control the aircraft well, the aircraft could swing from side to side the moment it landed. One must have a mastery of technique in order to land the DC-3 safely.

Sitting next to my cadets, I witnessed how their faces grew white during their first attempt at landing the aircraft. The moment the tailwheel touched the ground, the aircraft began wobbling out of control. Many of them were paralysed with the fear of crashing the aircraft that they did not know how to react. They forgot that I was also in control of the aircraft. And before anything went awry, I swiftly corrected the movement of the aircraft, and the DC-3 landed safely on the runway without any incident. Though we had landed safely, the experience was so incredibly nerve-wracking and risky for the cadets that many lost a lot of confidence after their first failed attempt at landing. Some were so shaken by the experience that they wanted to give up.

These incidences made me think back to my early days in Malayan Airways, at a time when the expatriate pilots used to treat the local pilots harshly. I remembered how these aggressive instructors used to intimidate the local cadets and placed them under such immense pressure that they could not perform the required tasks. Many were so demoralised that they dropped out of training in the end.

Now that I was a Training Captain, I was on a personal mission to increase the number of local pilots for the Airline. I was determined to train these cadets to the best of my abilities and imbue them with the confidence they needed to fly well. I understood how the fear of crashing could cause a cadet to freeze up and forget all that he needed to do high up in the air. And I had to ensure I did everything I could to boost their morale and their confidence.

After these incidences, I made it a point to always warmly greet my cadets and engage in hearty conversations before boarding the aircraft. Sometimes, I would talk to them about their families. Other times, I would talk about their ambitions and dreams. Conversations like these were useful, not only to help them relax their mind about training, but it was a great way for us to get to know each other better. And when we were done with training, I would take my cadets out for lunch where we could enjoy a hearty meal and a warm atmosphere of camaraderie.

It was through little gestures like these that I wanted my cadets to know that I was more than an instructor. I wanted them to know that they could look to me as a friend, as an equal, or even a close family figure that they could trust and turn to for help and advice. I wanted them to feel comfortable learning to fly with me in the cockpit. These efforts paid off, and as the days went by, I could see how much more relaxed and calmer they were in the cockpit, so much so that training had ceased to be a chore. It became an enjoyable experience that they looked forward to each day. They were eager and excited to learn, and their energy motivated me to share more of my flying experience, like the finer points of manoeuvering the DC-3.

Patience was the critical virtue of a good flight instructor. It was something I had to constantly practise each and every single day on the job. Whenever my cadets felt nervous or unsure, or if they made a mistake, I had to reassure them that they were doing fine. Sometimes, to distract them from their anxieties, I would share with them my experiences as a bomber pilot during the Second World War in China. I discovered that the stories of my own struggles as a pilot during the war inspired them to persevere and push on in their training.

What the cadets needed was to develop the confidence to handle the aircraft, and they needed plenty of opportunities to develop that confidence. By the time cadets had clocked about three to five hours of training, many could land the aircraft, and they became more confident flying the aircraft on their own.

My own confidence on my abilities as an instructor grew too, the more time I spent training cadets.

*\ *\ *

After some time as a Training Captain, I learnt that spending a few hours with a cadet was enough for me to gain a sense of the type of trainee I had to deal with. Some were naturals, almost as if they were born to fly. They were able to master control of the aircraft after only six hours of flight. Some others were steady learners. While they did not learn as fast as the naturals, their learning progressed steadily.

The last group were trainees that needed some 'hand-holding.' Like a father holding the hands of a toddler as he learns to walk, I was always by their side, holding their hands by vigilantly watching every move they made in the cockpit so as to prevent any mishap from occurring. They were clearly nervous. I had to constantly reassure them every step of the way that they were doing fine. And I patiently watched them progress slowly and steadily until they mastered the DC-3.

As much as possible, M. S. Leong and I tried not to fail any of them. They had spent so much time and energy to learn. We did not think it was right to dash their dreams of becoming a pilot. At the same time, we both were hoping to train more local pilots so that we could be proud of our national carrier for having more flights operated by local crew.

We were very patient with the weaker cadets. Some of them had a hard time mastering control over the aircraft, and they struggled a lot. We gave them extra time to practice, and M. S. was very happy to take them under his wing. In all my life, I have never met anyone as patient and gentle as him. M. S. had such a good nature, he never got angry, swore at anyone, or even scolded a person. He was, to me, a living saint. And it was thanks to his extraordinary patience that many of the weaker cadets became the best and most responsible pilots in the Airline.

* * *

After the cadets had completed fifteen hours of familiarisation through Base Training, they proceeded to the next stage, known as

'Line Training.' By this stage of the training, the cadets were very confident in flying the DC-3. This allowed me to focus our training on overseas flight routes, and to familiarise them with landmarks on the ground so that they could visually find airports during adverse weather conditions.

In particular, I enjoyed teaching my cadets how to find Ipoh Airport in Malaya. It was, after all, the town where M. S. Leong and I grew up. And we were very familiar with the landmarks and the terrain of Ipoh. Together, we developed a unique landing approach for finding the runway. The airport was situated in a valley surrounded by hills on the northern, southern, and eastern sides. One had to approach the airport from the western side of the hill. To do this, all one had to do was to descend to about 500 feet over the sleepy town of Batu Gajah and follow the canal. After passing over the fourth bridge, one had to head in a north-east direction, and the runway will be right ahead.

The cadets were very impressed with the unique techniques that M. S. Leong and I had developed. It also helped that I had stories for some of the major landmarks on the ground, as it made it easier for the cadets to remember and easily spot them from high up in the air.

One of my favourite destinations when we're out flying on Line Training was on the B737 Bangkok, Thailand. From Singapore, it was just a short two-hour flight away. And the airport ground facilities were readily available for training purposes, making Bangkok an ideal destination for training. Once done with our training, we would always make a bee-line to a popular cluster of restaurants serving good Thai food in Suriwong, which we affectionately dubbed, "M. S. Square" after M. S. Leong, where there was a cluster of restaurants. We were sure to have a grand feast there. It was on those evenings that we bonded very closely.

As much as possible, I strongly encouraged my cadets to get along well everyone, including the ground crew, cabin crew, and the air traffic control crew. I led by example, showing them how close I was to the air and ground crew in every airport we visited. In fact, we got along so well that on certain midnight flights to Kuala Lumpur, the air traffic staff there would even help us order food and brought it personally to our aircraft. It was nothing fancy, just a freshly cooked supper of *nasi lemak* (coconut milk steamed rice and served with chilli and side dishes). On a quick turnaround flight, it was comfort food at its finest, and a treat that the entire aircrew could enjoy together.

It was these little things that M. S. Leong and I did to help create a positive work culture and environment that helped the cadets to flourish under our wing. As the weeks went by, our rapport and camaraderie grew beyond the necessities of work. More than just friends, we were like a family.

*　*　*

Throughout my time as a Training Captain, I could not help but see my father acting through me. When I was young, he strongly emphasised the importance of culture and family ties. To him, it was important for each and every one to have a strong sense of belonging. And if we committed ourselves to a task, we were to persevere through all the hardships that came our way. We had to struggle and endure all the way to the end. Last but not least, my father emphasised just how important it was for us to be proud of the work we did, regardless of how menial it may be.

My father raised and nurtured us with affection, yet led us with a firm guiding hand in instilling these values in us. All through my life, I saw how important they were in guiding me through all of lives precious and difficult moments.

I guess it was my father's style of raising us that rubbed off on me, and I found myself applying a very fatherly approach in the way I instructed the cadets entrusted to my care. I nurtured and trained them as if they were my children.

It is perhaps no wonder that so many of the junior pilots and cadets affectionately called me, 'Daddy-O.'

Chapter 24

A STUDENT ONCE AGAIN

The relationship between Singapore and Malaysia did not last very long. The two separated after two years, and Singapore became an independent and sovereign nation on 9 August 1965.

The conflict between the two Governments manifested in more ways than one. They fought hard over the ownership of the Airline, each side periodically raising their stakes in the Airline. Eventually, the two governments displaced private shareholders such as the British Overseas Aviation Corporation and Qantas Empire Airways.

Eventually, both Governments held equal stakes in the Airline and had reached a stalemate. It was at this point that the Airline came under the joint ownership of the two Governments and was renamed to Malaysia-Singapore Airlines (MSA).

Yet, the battle was far from over. The two Governments had vastly different plans for the future of the Airline. In spite of all the turmoil that was going on in the background, the General Manager of Malaysia-Singapore Airlines, Keith Hamilton, and his vibrant management team, projected an image of stability and calm within the organisation. They did their best to ensure smooth operations of their flights.

The Airline continued to expand its operations, its fleet, and the number of destinations around the world. I was lucky to witness the expansion of the Airline in its most tangible form through the intake of new cadet pilots. Each year, the numbers grew larger and larger. This filled with me a great sense of accomplishment, as it allowed me to witness how I cultivated so many of our local boys into professional commercial pilots.

* * *

March 1967

While I was busy training pilots under my care, the thought crossed my mind that I should be a student once again. I found it ironic that I had studied in three different universities in my lifetime and did not possess a degree. I had been blaming the war for disrupting my studies. But I have since enjoyed two decades of peacetime. What excuse do I have not to study?

I knew it would be difficult to become a student again. It was a long time since I engaged in intense study. Age was catching up on me. Nonetheless, I thought it might be a worthwhile pursuit. The intellectual challenge and stimulation might do wonders to my mind.

I visited the University of Singapore, which was at that time, the only university on the island that taught in the English language. I was unsure what was required to gain admission into the most prestigious university of this country, so I brought the results for the matriculation examination to Hong Kong University, which I took back in 1940. Needless to say, the administrative lady serving me was speechless seeing such an old document, her eyes widely opened in bewilderment.

When she finally found the words to respond to me, she apologised profusely and told me that my results were 27 years old and quite out of date. The University would not accept these results. If I wanted to enrol to the University, I had to sit for a other entrance examination.

I was unsure what topics were covered as I had not studied for almost three decades. So I asked for some sample test papers. The administrative lady gladly obliged, and helped to retrieve a set for me.

I returned home that day with a new challenge. I was quite excited by this challenge, and I promptly rescheduled my appointments in order to study for the examination. It was not easy trying to juggle examination preparations with my work as a flight instructor.

In the day, I was training pilots. And in the evenings, I was training for the matriculation examination. My study sessions often crossed late into the night as there were so much that I needed to catch up in my learning. There were even times when I had to ask my cadets, who were still fresh out of school to help me with some of the more difficult topics. At first, they were bemused by my questions. How were questions about mathematics, current affairs, or even abstract concepts even relevant to the flying of a DC-3? They initially thought that I was testing them. But when my cadets finally understood that I was trying to matriculate into university, they were very happy to help. Some even offered to tutor me during our lunch breaks.

This period of preparation was incredibly arduous. The last time I worked this hard was when I was preparing for the Hong Kong University's matriculation examination. It certainly felt good to remember what it was like to be young as I recalled many nostalgic memories from the days of my youth.

Eventually, the day came for the entrance examination. My presence in the examination hall attracted many stares from parents, puzzled youths, as well as the confused invigilators. The test questions were really difficult. I was amazed that our youth were required to have such a high level of intellectual competency. It made me realised just how much times have changed, and how much smarter the next generation had become.

I left the examination hall feeling rather downcast. I did not think that I would do well enough to be accepted into the University. I walked out consoling myself that I had put up a good fight in the weeks before, and that itself was a worthwhile experience.

* * *

August 1967

The University of Singapore

It was the first day of classes at the University of Singapore. There I sat in the middle of the huge lecture theatre, wondering how on earth did I make it here?

Months ago, I received the results of the entrance examination. To my surprise and to the surprise of my family and colleagues, I had passed the examination and was accepted into the University of Singapore's Faculty of Arts to study Political Science and Sociology. I was quite proud of the achievement. I did not think that it was possible for a man of my age to have made it for what seemed like an impossible test.

I continued sitting in the lecture theatre in disbelief of what had happened. Was this a dream?

My presence in the lecture theatre attracted many curious stares. There, sitting in the middle of the lecture theatre was a middle-aged man. I certainly stood out like a sore thumb. The students too were in disbelief. How could someone at my age be a student? Some thought that I was a parent accompanying his child on the first day of school. Many others thought that I was the lecturer trying to pull a prank on the class. But as it turns out, the lecturer entered the lecture theatre, and he was much younger than I was.

The students were shocked!

As luck would have it, Prime Minister Lee Kuan Yew was on campus that day for his annual visit around the University. He entered the lecture theatre that I was in. Everyone inside was taken aback by his sudden appearance. The room became so silent, you could hear a pin drop.

Prime Minister Lee spotted me seated amidst hundreds of students. His face held an expression of disbelief. He pointed at me, saying, "You… You… You…"

Everyone was worried. Was I about to get into trouble with the most fearsome political leader of the country?

It was clear the Prime Minister was trying to recall who I was. A few seconds later, he remembered and he called out from across the lecture theatre, "You… Aren't you Captain Ho? Why aren't you flying?"

I was very elated to see that he remembered me after so many years. I happily responded, "I'm trying to get a degree at 50!"

He was very pleased to hear it, and also rather amused. As he left the lecture theatre, he encouraged me to do my best, and he wished me well for my studies.

Many students in the lecture theatre were astonished by what they had witnessed. There were whispers in the crowds, "Who is this man? Why does our Prime Minister know him?"

After class, four young men approached me. They introduced themselves as Heng Chiang Meng, Karmjit Singh, Chen Chun Chan, and Kong Heng Yew. They were curious about me and how I ended up in their class as a student. I was happy to share my story with them. Since then, we became good friends and we spent a lot of time together over meals and studies.

* * *

As it turns out, studying was a lot tougher than I imagined. I don't remember my time at the Hong Kong University to be this intense. There were a lot of readings, and the assignments required me to carry out research. This was an almost impossible feat as I had to compete with the other students for access to library books. By the time I was able to make my way to the library, the books were all gone from the shelves. And even if I was able to find a book I needed, there was always a long queue of students waiting to check-out the books with the librarian. My tight schedule did not allow me the luxury of waiting in line. I had to give up the hope of borrowing the books I needed.

To make matter worse, I still had my work and family commitments to attend to. My daily routine involved me waking up early in the morning to drop my kids off at school before coming to the University for lessons. Once classes were done, I had to rush off to Paya Lebar Airport to conduct flight training for the new intake of cadets.

Evenings were the only time I had to read and catch up on my assignments. But even that was a scarce resource as I often had to tend to my wife and children.

There were some occasions where I had to fly overseas and spend a night in the hotel. On those days, I brought my books and notes with me.

I struggled through the entire academic year. But thankfully I had the assistance of my four good friends whom I could rely on for help. They understood how difficult it was for someone my age to cope with the fast pace of studies, and they did all they could to help me. Whenever I asked to borrow their notes, they were more than willing to make copies for me. They certainly helped to alleviate the stress of being a middle-aged student.

* * *

August 1968

I survived a whole academic year. It certainly wasn't easy at all, and I was indebted to the kindness and help of my four friends. It was certainly good fun experiencing life as a student once again, and I was glad I did. But after all the difficulty that I had to go through, I decided that I was way past my prime to be a student. And with a heavy heart, I withdrew from the University.

I understood now how the younger generation was so much better than I was in so many aspects. I respected their amazing abilities. I decided I was better off concentrating my efforts at training the next generation of pilots. I had the full confidence that they will succeed me and do a much better job in the future for the Airline.

Chapter 25

TURBULENCE

The late 1960s and early 1970s were a turbulent time for everyone in Malaysian Airways. The two Governments had vastly different plans for the future of the Airline. The Malaysian Government wanted to focus on developing its domestic routes. The Singapore Government, on the other hand, wanted to develop the Airline's international routes. This led to many conflicts and disagreements until January 1971, when the two Governments decided it was best to break up the Airline.

But even the breakup of the Airline was itself a point of contention. The initials, MSA, was a brand that was internationally recognised, and both Governments wanted to retain the initials for themselves. The Singapore Government initially proposed the name, "Mercury Singapore Airlines," as a tribute to the founder of Singapore, Sir Stamford Raffles (Mercury was the name of the ship he used to sail to Singapore). This proposal, of course, angered the Malaysian Government.

In the end, the two Governments agreed not to fight over the prized initials. And on 1 October 1972, the Airline was split into Singapore Airlines (SIA) and Malaysian Airline System (MAS).

Separation was a slow and agonising process for everyone on both sides. During this tumultuous period of change, a vast majority of local pilots had expressed their intention to join Malaysian Airline System. This meant a large reduction in the strength of our aircrew in Singapore Airlines, and especially those precious local talent which M. S. Leong and I worked so hard to build up. It was sad having to bid farewell to some of our best and most promising pilots.

The exodus of pilots placed Singapore Airlines in a rather difficult position. The management wanted to rapidly expand its international routes, but we had a shortage of qualified pilots to service those routes. The Government of Singapore set up its own flying school in Seletar to provide basic flight training for the newly recruited cadets. And in the meantime, the Airline had no choice but to hire new expatriate pilots to make up for the loss in numbers.

* * *

April 1973

Many changes rolled out in Singapore Airlines, and I soon found myself becoming part of that change itself. The Airline promoted me to the role of Chief Pilot of the Boeing 737 commercial jets. As Chief Pilot, my duties and responsibilities were far greater than that of a Training Captain. I was in charge of a team of flight instructors and all the aircrew that flew the B-737 aircraft. I still conducted flight training from time to time. Beyond that, I had to also plan their future career progression. This meant that I was constantly on the lookout to identify pilots in my fleet who showed the potential to be commanders. Once identified, I had to nurture them through my regular interactions with them, and provide opportunities so that they could demonstrate their potential for leadership.

Identifying future commanders was a task I had to do with the great caution. Once someone was promoted, you cannot take it back without facing a massive backlash. I was always on the lookout for certain qualities, like how well they coped in simulated emergencies during training, how well they complied with safety regulations, how they made decisions, and the timing and manner of their execution.

* * *

Young pilots came under my care twice in their career. The first time was when they started out as cadets, where I had to show them how to fly a commercial aircraft. The second time was after they had been identified as suitable candidates for command training. It was my role to cultivate in them the qualities of a good commander.

Many pilots came back to me after serving five or six years in the Airline. Seeing them again after so many years left me with a deep sense of wonder. I remembered each and every single one of them vividly because of the close interactions we had during weeks of training while they were still cadets. Most pilots were surprised that I still remembered them and the many stories they shared with me years ago. I regarded them as my own children, and I made it a point to remember all that they shared with me, just like my own children did at home.

For the command training programme, I saw it of paramount importance to instil in them the qualities of a good leader. These soon-to-be commanders had to learn how to carry themselves with the right deportment so as to inspire confidence in both their crew and passengers. I showed them how to effectively manage and communicate with the crew, both in regular times and especially so in times of emergencies.

Above all, I emphasised how important it was to be humble and considerate to one's subordinates and everyone else in the Airline. These were the essential qualities of good leadership, and I found myself often repeating an old saying: "You cannot demand respect. You command respect by respecting others."

I had seen many commanders engulfed by the allure of the prestigious rank. In their insecure desire to be respected by others, they pulled their rank around only to receive treatment that made them feel more insecure. At times, the prestige of the rank can transform pilots to become so over-confident of themselves, that they were prone to making reckless decisions that made life a living hell for themselves and the poor people under them. I know this as I had been on the receiving end of such treatment. No one should have to experience this at all.

Humility and kindness are key qualities that a leader needs to have in order to continue building a friendly and trusting work culture and environment. No organisation could ever do well in the long-term without it. Trust is a very fragile thing, and it is paramount for a commander to preserve the trust in his team. Once damaged, it is very difficult for a commander to restore.

To impress this point in them, I myself led by example so that these pilots could see for themselves the importance of such qualities in leadership, and the fruits it bore when one were to conduct one's self in such a manner. It created an environment where we could trust and depend on each other. We accommodated to each other's needs and wants with a positive attitude of 'give-and-take.' Most of all, there was always a sense of professional mutual respect. That was a respect that a commander needed to learn to cultivate on his own.

Apart from inculcating important qualities of good leadership, I had to train these pilots to resolve problems and to make quick and important decisions under duress. Everyone's lives are in the hands of the commander once the aircraft had taken off. It is a heavy responsibility to bear, and so it is critical to be able to make the right decisions in stressful situations. The right decision could mean the safety and well-being of the crew and passengers.

Much of command training took place in the air. I accompanied the pilots on routine commercial flights to observe how they handled a variety of situations and tasks as commander-to-be, and I gave feedback on what the pilots had done. I found it important to praise the pilot for all the things he did right, just as it was vital to highlight mistakes and offer feedback on how he could have done it better.

When they had met the minimum hours of training, and satisfied all the requirements of command training, I was ready to 'check out' the pilot. In other words, to pass the pilot from command training and promote him to the esteemed rank of Captain.

* * *

Bik Gurm and Ken Toft were among the first batch of cadets I trained. They were star performers, and they rose through the ranks very quickly. I was very honoured to receive them as the first pilots to undergo command training under me. Eventually, the time came when I knew they were ready to be 'checked out.'

We have a very special tradition in Singapore Airlines when it was time for the instructor to 'check out' a pilot. We would usually perform this tradition on flights where the aircraft had a few stopovers.

Just before the pilot and I were about to board the aircraft to head to the next airport, I would stop the pilot, and take out from my pocket a set of new epaulettes bearing four golden bars (signifying the Captain's rank). I would help the newly promoted Captain to put on the new epaulettes on his shoulders. And with that, I would look at him and say, "Captain, you're on your own now. I'll see you back in Singapore."

I would then stay behind at the airport to catch the next flight, while the newly-promoted Captain would embark on his maiden voyage as a commander.

I fondly remembered carrying out this tradition for the first time with Bic Gurm and Ken Toft. It was an incredibly heart-warming moment for us. I remember seeing how grateful they were when I called them Captain for the first time. They were filled with so much pride and joy.

It reminded me of the importance of my personal mission to train local pilots. I wasn't just training local pilots to merely fly aeroplanes for Singapore Airlines. I was forming a whole generation of commanders who would take our national airline to great heights. I was part of that crucial process in shaping and moulding them to become good, dependable, and responsible commanders. And I was very proud of every single one I trained, as they have come to be well-respected pilots all over the world.

* * *

One day, I was in my office in Paya Lebar Airport, when suddenly Charlie Chan, who was now the Director of Flight Operations, burst into my room looking very worried. He told me that one of our aircraft had a failed engine and was making its way back for an emergency landing.

We rushed to the men's toilet, as it had a clear view of the runway. Some of the Airline's top management were there too. The window was, unfortunately, rather small, and so several of them were pushing and shoving to get a view of the situation.

Charlie feared the worst. If the aircraft crashed, it would be a huge disaster for the Airline. His head would be on the chopping block. He asked me, "Didn't you just promote Tony Tan to a Captain yesterday. He's returning from his maiden voyage as commander. He's so new. Are you sure he'll be ok?"

I was confident in my assessment. I had very high standards for my pilots and I would only pass them if I was very sure they could handle emergencies like a failed engine. I looked at Charlie and assured him, "I passed Tony. I know he's ok. Don't worry about it."

I was not anxious, and I certainly did not want to fight for a glimpse of the runway. Instead, I stood aside and listened to the few at the window commenting on the problematic B-737 aircraft as it fast approached the runway.

In the end, Captain Tony Tan succeeded in landing the aircraft safely on the runway without any incident, with everyone in the toilet cheering with applause. I was very proud of Tony that day. I knew he could make a successful landing.

***

February 1974

Being a Chief Pilot was not always a bed of roses. I constantly found myself in a difficult situation. I was considered a part of the management team, and that put me regularly at odds with the Pilots'

Association. Now known as the Singapore Airlines Pilots' Association, this was the very same association I had founded with several other local pilots when the Airline was once Malayan Airways. After two decades, the association had grown to over 2000 members, and I was very proud of what it had become. However, now that I was Chief Pilot, I was not permitted to attend the association's regular meetings to prevent any potential conflict of interests.

The pilot's association had their own priorities and their own policies. Oftentimes it aligned with the Airline's own priorities and direction. But when it did not, it was a very difficult position for me to be in. On one hand, I was expected to serve the Airline's broader interests, yet on the other hand, I found myself in a dilemma as I often sympathised more with the local pilots, many of whom I had nurtured and trained when they were cadets.

This time, the pilots had an industrial dispute against the Airline. The association was unhappy that pilots' wages did not increase with the times, and they were upset that not enough local pilots were given the opportunity for leadership.

I sympathised with my fellow pilots' dissatisfaction. But as Chief Pilot, I was not allowed to involve myself in the fight. On matters of leadership, I could only give strong recommendations on who should be promoted from within my fleet, and I fought hard for their promotion at the high-level meetings. But for everything else, it was up to my fellow pilots in the association. All I could do was to encourage my fellow pilots to fight hard for what they believed in.

* * *

28 April 1975

Saigon, Vietnam

Looking through the window of my Boeing 737 cockpit, I could see in the distance, several South Vietnamese fighter jets circling around Tan Son Nhut Airport. As my aircraft drew closer to the runway, the jets made a small gap, big enough for my aircraft to pass through and land on the runway.

As I began the descent of the aircraft, I radioed to the rest of my crew to prepare for landing. Once we were on the ground, we had a fifteen-minute window to carry out the evacuation. The atmosphere within the aircraft was tense. While my crew were familiar with evacuation procedures, they were not mentally prepared for what we were about to do.

We only got word of the mission in the morning.

*　*　*

Earlier in the day, the South Vietnamese Embassy in Singapore contacted Singapore Airlines to relay a special request from its Vice President Nguyen Cao Ky. The Viet Cong forces had broken through Saigon's outer defences and they were closing in on the city. Vice President Nguyen, who was also the Chief of the Air Force, was pessimistic about the outcome. He predicted that Saigon would fall in a matter of days. He needed our help to evacuate two bishops out of Saigon. One of them, we were told was wheelchair bound and could not move easily. To ensure our safety during evacuation, Vice President Nguyen had ordered the air force to circle and protect the airport.

Singapore Airlines agreed to lend a helping hand and issued a request for pilots to be involved in this mission. I immediately stepped forward. I had flown many perilous missions in China during the Second World War, and so I was very confident of my flying abilities in a situation like this. And as Chief Pilot, I knew precisely who I could rely on in my crew to carry out the evacuation swiftly. I put together a special evacuation team, and in less than an hour we were up in the air, on our way to Saigon.

* * *

The moment the B-737 aircraft landed on the runway, my crew jumped into action. We could hear the sounds of gunfire and explosions faintly from a distance. The sounds brought me back to the days of the war. We were very anxious and fearful of being hit by enemy artillery fire. Many in my crew were young, fresh out of school. This was their first exposure to war.

There was supposed to be two bishops. But on the runway, we met just one — Bishop Carlo Joseph Van Melckebeke, the religious leader of the Catholics in Ningxia, China. He had a broken arm and sat quite frailly on his wheelchair. Due to religious persecution from the Communists, he fled China and sought refuge in Saigon where he stayed with the Archbishop of Saigon, Paul Nguyen Van Binh.

The Archbishop of Saigon was nowhere to be seen on the runway. He had refused Vice President Nguyen's opportunity to evacuate, insisting instead on staying behind with his followers.

Within ten minutes, my crew had settled Bishop Van Melckebeke on board the aircraft, and we took off immediately.

We returned to Singapore safely that day without any mishap.

The next day, I learnt that the Viet Cong forces had advanced further into Saigon and destroyed the runway of Tan Son Nhut Airport. And on 30 April 1975, Saigon had fallen to the Communists.

As a pilot, I was involved in many special missions of evacuating people and bodies. But of all the missions I was involved in, this was the most memorable one as a civilian pilot.

* * *

17 September 1977

Mount Alvernia Hospital, Singapore

Gus had been fighting a long hard battle against lung cancer. It pained me to watch her suffer so much. We travelled overseas in search for treatment, but none had much of an effect on her. She showed no signs of recovery. As her husband, it was painful for me to watch her physically deteriorate with my own eyes. Each day, she grew weaker and weaker. By this time, she was unable to speak. She could barely move.

Her struggle made me so painfully aware that I will soon lose the very love of my life. It was a horrible thought that kept playing through my mind again and again. I was afraid of losing her.

Each night, I accompanied Gus in the medical ward. I sat next to her and held her cold hands tightly in mine. I felt a strong sense of helplessness. I did not know what else to do but to pray.

Last night, I tried something different. I recorded a message on tape for Gus, hoping that my voice could provide her some comfort. I bore my feelings to her, consoled her, and thanked her for such a wonderful and faithful wife. I played the recording over and over again, as I held her hands tightly in mine just to let her know that I was right beside her. She could not respond; her body would not allow her to do so. But deep inside me, I knew that she was grateful for the gesture.

Today, Gus breathed her last.

It pained me so much to see Gus go. Losing the precious love of my life was like losing a huge part of myself. I had lost my closest and greatest friend. I was grief-stricken. Words could not express my immense sorrow. I cried that night.

While I grieved over her departure, I felt a sense of relief knowing that Gus did not have to endure the suffering anymore.

*　*　*

Life continues despite the absence of a loved-one. I decided to dedicate all my time and energy to the welfare and care of the pilots under me. Despite the responsibilities of being a Chief Pilot, I made myself available to anyone who needed help one way or another. I kept a constant lookout for the weakest cadets in my fleet and personally took charge of their training. I always believed they should be given a second chance, especially since they succeeded in making it this far. Naturally, they were quite intimidated that a Chief Pilot personally oversaw their training. But as the days went by, we bonded very well. I felt as though I was brought back to the simpler days where I was just a Training Captain.

At times, distressed cadets came to see me as they felt they had problems with their instructors. As much as possible, I tried not to intervene between them as I trusted that my instructors were doing their very best. But since I knew my instructors well, I was able to give my cadets advice on how to work well with them, so that they could learn how to handle interpersonal problems on their own. They were very grateful for the advice, and I was very pleased to see them make much progress after that.

Once again, the familiar name, "Daddy-O," surfaced regularly in my interactions with them. I saw my father acting through me, as I myself became a fatherly figure within my fleet, tending to the pilots whom I regarded as part of my family.

Gus would have been proud of what I had accomplished.

Chapter 26

MANY HAPPY LANDINGS

21 March 1980

This was the day I turned 60 years old. This was my last day of work, and it ended quite spectacularly.

I had just landed the B-737 aircraft at Paya Lebar Airport. It was the last flight of my aviation career. Upon stepping into the airport, I was greeted by my pilot friends. As part of the Airline's tradition for celebrating one's retirement, one of them grabbed hold of my necktie and snipped it off with a pair of scissors.

That evening, the Flight Operations Division organised a really huge retirement party, and I was surrounded by so many pilots that I had trained over the years. I had clocked over 20,000 hours of flying, and I trained more than 300 pilots, all of whom formed the core flying team of Singapore Airlines. For the longest time, I had a vague sense that I had trained many pilots and they went on to contribute significantly to help the Airline succeed with its rapid expansion internationally.

During my conversation with the pilots, I was amazed by how far they had come. Some had been so inspired by my training that they too decided to become flight instructors. They were so proud to have me as their instructor that they even introduced me to their cadets as the 'Daddy-O' of Singapore Airlines. Some of them joked that I was the 'grandfather' of the Airline. Most had been posted to other fleets as commanders. But more importantly, so many of the pilots I trained had gone on to fly the Boeing 747 aircraft, which helped propel Singapore Airlines to international fame.

It was incredible to look at these pilots and realise how I had touched and transformed so many lives as a flight instructor. I thoroughly enjoyed the role as I found great satisfaction in passing my knowledge and experience to younger pilots.

I loved flying. I had developed so many great and lasting friendships because of it. In particular was my close childhood friend and colleague, M. S. Leong. It's simply incredible how we have been together since our childhood days. Our colleagues nicknamed us, "the twins," because of how much we resembled each other from a distance, and how we both shared the same sense of humour.

Of all the friendships I made, the ones I felt closest to were the ones whom I shared the experience of flying during the Second World War in China. We had a strong unspoken bond forged from the hardships of war. War had brought out both the best and the worst of us. And yet, in spite of all that, we were still brothers always on the lookout for one another.

Like all good things in life, my exciting flying career and all the adventures that accompanied me came to an end with my retirement from Singapore Airlines.

EPILOGUE

Life for me has been one long struggle. My father taught me well the importance of enduring through the struggles in life. It is always worth putting up a fight if it is for a good cause. It is easy to become complacent and feel directionless when everything in life feels comfortable.

But because of the hardships I had to endure, I spent my entire life fighting against oppression and discrimination. During the war, I fought to free China from its oppressors. And during my career as a commercial pilot, I fought so that local pilots could have equal opportunities. Nobody should be bullied because they are weak. Nobody should be bullied because they are different. I am proud for what I have fought for in my life.

Now, at the ripe old age of 99, the people I meet often ask me what is the secret to a long and healthy life?

The truth is, there is no secret to a long and healthy life, no formula or recipe of sorts. I just keep my body active in my younger days with a variety of sports, such as golf and tennis. And to keep my mind active, not only did I play games like bridge regularly, but I made it a point to visit all my old friends scattered around the world. I love to engage with people, whether over conversation or through an activity. I draw my strength and meaning from the people I meet. And especially old friends whom I have not met for a long time. The thought of seeing them again excites me so much, I feel young again just thinking back to my younger days with them.

People also ask me if I have found the answer to happiness since I have lived for so long. I spent the prime years of my life searching for happiness. I tried to find happiness in all kinds of things. I thought that I could be happy if I secured a good education. But that got taken away from me. I thought that I could be happy if I found love. But even that got taken away from me, multiple times. I thought that I could be happy if I could find a sense of belonging with my historical and cultural roots. But that got taken away from me too.

I struggled long and hard to find the answer to happiness only to find such happiness fleeting. Eventually, I found the answer, and it had been something I spent my entire life doing all along. And it was best expressed by Dr. Frank Crane who wrote:

> "Happiness is great love and much service. If you will look about carefully among the people you know, not neglecting yourself, you will discover that not one of them is happy that does not love. Furthermore, that all of them are happy in proportion as they love.
>
> Happiness is the perfume of the rose of love, the light shining from the candle of love, the sound from the bells of love.
>
> You can get a certain something that resembles happiness from the gratification of desire, from eating, drinking, playing, and the like. But it all has in itself the seed of boredom. You get SATED from satisfying your appetite; but in the happiness that comes from love is no satiety.
>
> What is true of love is equally true of service; because to love is to serve. Search again among the people you know, and note that they are happy in proportion as they serve.

The great mass of men and women are reasonably content because they are at work. They often complain of their work. They even call labor a curse. But they would be miserable without it.

They dream of a life of idleness and self-indulgence, and many imagine that is heaven. It is not. It is hell.

The world was made for lovers and servants.

If anyone's heart is full of love, and his hand is full of service, he has no morbid 'problems.' He has solved the riddle of life."

All my life, I had a passion for helping people. I was happiest when I was in their service, giving my time to make a difference to their day, and even to their lives. Since the day I read Dr Crane's passage, I realised that my life's calling was in helping others as a pilot. While I was indeed passionate about flying, I was even more passionate about helping others in a variety of ways through flying. This gave me a sense of purpose, a mission, and fulfilment.

And though I am now retired, I still derive that happiness from the people I meet. Whether it is a chance to catch up with old friends, spend time with my family, or even to meet someone new, I draw strength and joy from meeting them precisely because of the exciting prospects of forging a closer bond, or the chance to lend a helping hand or a listening ear.

I spent my entire life searching for happiness and I found it in helping the people I loved.

This is my story.

PHOTOS

YOUNGER DAYS IN IPOH

The Ho Family gathering at my father's birthday in Ipoh, Malaysia, 1970

Family portriat, with me standing second from left, Ipoh, Malaya, 1929

Younger Days in Ipoh

I am standing third from left with my parents and siblings, Ipoh, Malaya, 1926

With my mother, second sister Mary, me and younger brother Weng Kong, Ipoh, Malaya, 1932

During my school days at St Michael's Institution, I was active in the scout group. Here I am standing in the second row, 4th from left. Ipoh, Malaya, 1935

As a teenager in Ipoh, Malaya, 1936

Younger Days in Ipoh   221

My 4th Uncle Ho Kok Yew, extreme right, was instrumental for sponsoring me for further studies in Hong Kong, Ipoh, Malaya, 1932

Portrait of my father, Ho Kok Lim and mother Chow Kheng Sin. My father came from Guandong to Malaya in 1902 at age 16 and later set up shoe business in Ipoh

Photo of me just before leaving Ipoh for further studies in Hong Kong, 1938

PREWAR HONG KONG

Student at St Stephen's College Stanley, Hong Kong, 1939

Photo taken just after Japanese occupation of Hong Kong. Back row from left: me, MS Leong, Doong Siew Ming, Eddie Yan. Seated, from left: Loretta Ng, Lily Li and Nelly Woo, 1942

Prewar Hong Kong

Seated 2nd from right, with a group of Perak students at Hong Kong University, just months before WWII, Hong Kong, 1941

In the summer of 1942, I fled Hong Kong with a group of 25 Hong Kong University students. After several days of arduous journey we reached Kukong, the wartime capital of Guangdong Province

With Lau Hun Ming my St Stephen's College roommate, Stanley, Hong Kong, 1939

CHINESE AMERICAN COMPOSITE WING (CACW)

In our standby duties attire, standing in front of our 1st Bomb Squadron, Chinese American Composite Wing insignia, the Monkey God emblem, Hanchung, China, 1945

2nd Lt Winfred Bird Liason Officer for CACW cadets. I remained friends with him and his family after WWII

Group of newly commissioned B25 officers at La Juanta US Air Force Base, Colorado, 1944

After a combat mission, Hanchung, China, 1944

B25 Formation, 1944

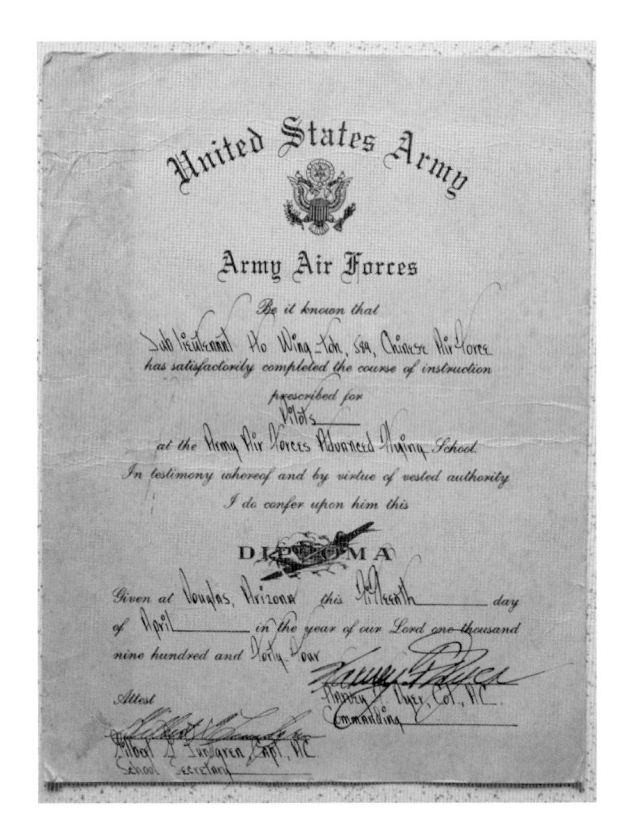

My hard earned USAAF Diploma, 15 April, 1944

Chinese American Composite Wing (CACW) 231

Portrait of taken just after WWII, 1945

The entire 1st Bomb Squadron celebrating the Japanese surrender, Hanchung, China, 1945

Posing with Samurai swords just after Japanese surrender, Hankow, China, 1945

In Chinese Air Force Ceremonal Uniform, 1945

Chinese American Composite Wing (CACW) 233

Kasun Chu Pee my Tibetan buddy of Chinese Air Force Class 16, 1944

After my first training flight on the Steerman at Thunderbird Field Glendale, Arizona, USA, 1943

With squadron mates Bill Carroll, centre and Frankie Kan, far right. After the war they became a lawyer and doctor respectively. Hanchung, China, 1945

As a cadet at the Marana USAAF Base, Arizona, USA, 1943

Chinese American Composite Wing (CACW) 235

At the controls of a B25; cockpit view, 1944

With Col. Peter Chung, fellow Ipoh boy, 1945

236　　　　　　　　　*Memoirs of a Flying Tiger*

With members of United States Army Air Forces class 44D pilots celebrating the successful completion of 1 year of combat missions, at Hangchung Air Base, China, 1945

Yau Sau Wah, Chinese Air Force P41 Ace Pilot, a fellow Ipoh boy, who later became a commercial pilot with Malayan Airways, 1945

# POST WWII

In 1948, I reconnected with Eleanor Eu in Shanghai. She was studying to be a doctor in the Shanghai Medical College. We remain close friends till today

After leaving the Chinese Air Force, I joined Central Air Transport Corporation as a First Officer and flew to many cities in China from our base in Shanghai, 1947

Post WWII 239

Graduation of pioneer batch of Central Air Transport Corporation Flight Stewardess, Shanghai, 1948

Painting the town red with Chinese Air Force buddy, Lee Yung Run, Shanghai, 1945

With some Hong Kong University students from Malaya who survived WWII. Standing from left, Dr Khoo kee Siang, Lau Seng Thung, Dr Saw Hock Chuan. Seated MS Leong, me, Dr Yeoh Seng Tung and Fong Yew Weng, December 1945

I meet Sook Fun most unexpectedly in 1947 at a bookstore in Shanghai. We had totally lost contact for over some 10 years

Standing at Birch Clock Tower with my brothers, from left: Weng Tuck, Weng Kong, Weng Keong and Weng Tai, after returning from China on home visit, Ipoh, Malaya, 1947

Meeting with students at the Raffles Medical School

MALAYAN AIRWAYS LIMITED (MAL)

1st Batch MAL Air Hostess, 1950

With Danny Fenton, MAL 1st Chief Pilot, Singapore, 1951

Malayan Airways Limited (MAL) 245

At dinner with some pioneer MAL pilots, 1957

Joined MAL in 1951 and flew the DC-3s

Appointed DC-3 Captain on 8 December 1961

MALAYSIA SINGAPORE AIRLINES (MSA)

On 3 Apr 1968, I took delivery of a new Fokker Friendship (F-27 Dutch-built aircraft) registration 9V-BBF. With First Officer Mohd Khairi, we took about 30 hours to fly from Amsterdam to Singapore; making several stops on the way. Khairi, later became Director of Flight Operations with Malaysian Airline System

With some senior Malaysian Airline System pilots that I trained; Standing from left: Ong Boo Hong, Simon Er, Saffian. Seated from left: Arshad Bakern and Ajuthen Puthiera. Kuala Lumpur, Malaysia, 1998

Malaysia Singapore Airlines (MSA) 249

F-27 with Malayan Airways Limited logo, 1969

F-27 with Malaysian Singapore Airlines logo, just before the airline split in October 1972, Singapore

With Malaysia Singapore Airlines before the airline split in October 1972

On 15 Aug 1969 I obtained my captaincy on the B737 after receiving flight training with Boeing

SINGAPORE AIRLINES (SIA)

When I retired from Singapore Airlines in 1980, I had clocked more than 20,000 hours

I spent many memorable years in the cockpit and witnessed the vast rapid developments of SIA in becoming a world leading airline

Singapore Airlines (SIA)

I was SIA B737 Chief Pilot from 1974 to 1980

Maintained links with SIA by being actively involved with the SIA Retirees Association

With my buddy MS Leong on a VIP Flight, Bali 1975

In 1972, when Malaysia Singapore Airlines split, I moved over to SIA

FAMILY

Celebrating our 25th Wedding Anniversary at the Singapore Cricket Club, 5 May 1974

Our wedding day, 5 May 1949, Shanghai

Augusta, right with younger sister, Alberta, Hankow, 1947

Augusta at Lung Hua Airport, Shanghai, 1948

Our Engagement, Shanghai, 1949

MS and Ann welcome Augusta on her first trip to Hong Kong, 1949

Augusta's parents, Jose and Anna Rodrigues, Hong Kong, 1956

Augusta carrying David, our new addition to the family, with Catherine and Fred beside her, Singapore, 1962

With daughter Catherine at my 98th birthday dinner, Singapore, 2018

With my family members, from left, Tim (SIL), daughter Catherine, Ruby (DIL), eldest son Fred, youngest son David, Mary (DIL) and grandsons, Damien and Daryl, 2015

Family 261

With son Fred and daughter-in-law Ruby at my 98th birthday dinner, Singapore, 2018

FRIENDS

Sr Agnes and Sr Thomasina of the Franciscan Missionaries of the Divine Motherhood with my second son David. He was born on 29 January 1962, at Mt Alvernia Hospital, Singapore

My son David and I, attending Sr Thomasina's Golden Anniversary of religious life. We have 60 plus years of friendship with the FMDM Sisters

I met Jenny Auw while a student in Hong Kong in 1939. Today, after 80 years, we are still in touch. In 2018 she made a special trip to Singapore celebrate my 98th birthday

With my dear friend Loretta during my visit to USA, 1994

Loretta Ng when I first knew her, Hong Kong, 1941

With Moon Chin the Chinese legiondary pilot, who mentored many China National Aviation Corporation pilots in the 1940s, Nanjing 2009

Friends

With my best buddy MS Leong, just after WWII, 1945

With MS on one of our many trips together, St Catalina Island, California, 1984

At Winfred Bird's home in Seattle, Washington, USA, 1968

With Viola, wife of Winfred Bird, USA, 1994

Visiting Ann and Albert Awana in USA. Albert was a hot CACW pilot from Hawaii. We spent lots of time together in our Hanchung air base and later after the war in Shanghai, while we were flying with Central Air Transport Corporation, California, 1968

Wishing you many happy landings

Fred Gurwitz, a GI whom I knew in 1944 while based in Hanchung 1944. We became close friends and visited him in USA several times. 1994

Godsons, from left Kok Seng, Robert, Justin, and Adrian, Singapore, 1983

With my regular "Tuesday Walkers", Singapore, 2015

Having dinner with Robert Kuok, Hong Kong, 2013

Get together with some of my golfing buddies, 2018

Visited cemetery where Marilyn Sweeney was buried, La Junta, Colorado, USA, 2002

Willie Ho and and wife, Hong Kong, 1972

With my dear friend Florence, whom I first met while we were students in Hong Kong University some 78 years ago. Hong Kong, 2017

With Gordon Poon, left and Peter Ho, Beijing, 1980

With Paul and Elaine Wan. Met Elaine during my flights to Penang in the 1960s. With my encouragement she took the plunge and came to Singapore with only $90. Singapore, 2010

Friends 275

With Peter Fong, London, 1972

At the wedding of YW Fong and Dianna, Shanghai, 1950

Some Airtrust staff celebrating my birthday, 2000

With my Airtrust friends, Linda, left and Evelyn, 2015

The "China Connection" pilots. From left, Fred Lin, Tommy Soong, Peter Fong, MS, and YW. Singapore, 1999

Maniam, master of ceremony at my 90th birthday, 2010

FLYING TIGERS CONVENTION

With Howard Halla, left at a Flying Tigers Convention in Arlington, Virginia, USA, 2005

With Bill Carroll, my Chinese American Composit Wing Hanchung comrade, attending Flying Tigers Return to China Tour to commemorate the 50th Anniversary of VJ Day, Beijing, 1995

Flying Tigers Convention 281

Receiving the Ding Hao Masters Golf trophy at a Flying Tigers Convention, San Antonio, Texas, USA, 1998

Reminiscing our 1st Bomb Squadron days with Howard Halla, centre and his neighbour, California, USA, 2002

Reunion with some members of 1st Bomb Squadron Chinese American Composite Wing at the 58th Flying Tigers Convention, Arlinton, Virgina, USA, 2005

At my first Flying Tigers Convention, Long Beach, Calfornia, 1990

Flying Tigers Convention 283

Remnants of the 1st Bomb Squadron, Chinese American Composit Wing, at the 51st Flying Tigers Convention in San Antonio, Texas, USA, 1998

With some Chinese Air Force coursemates, Taipei, 1985

EVENTS

Being presented with an appreciation plaque at the Hainanese Association after giving a talk on WWII, Singapore, 2016

At our annual family Christmas party, held at our 10 Bo Seng Ave home, Singapore, December, 1983

With some former senior SIA commanders that I trained in the 1960s celebrating my 99th Birthday. From left: Laurence, TW, Victor, Liew and KE, 2019

With Dr San Gupta (2nd from right) of Singapore Anti-Tuberculosis Association and friends at a Hong Kong University Alumni Dinner, Singapore, 1956

Attending dinner with Bishop Melckebeke, seated extreme right, followed by me, my wife and Fr DeBlowee (4th from right), Singapore, circa 1960

SPORTS

15th Asean Snr Amateur Open Golf Tournament, Thailand, 1997

With golfing friends, Seah Guan Chye, left and Tiger Wong, extreme right, 1993

Competing in the 5th Beijing International Veteran's Tennis Tournament, 1991

Receiving Tennis Trophy at Singapore Cricket Club, circa 1968

With my Singapore Cricket Club Tennis friends, from left: George Suppiah, Alsogolf, and Dr Tom Huges, cicra 1968

With partner Peter Fong after winning the Singapore International Philips Tennis Open Doubles, 1989

With some Singapore Cricket Club Billiard players, 1970s

With my tennis trophies, circa 1979

Winner of the Tanglin Club 3 Ball Billiards Tournament, flanked by Ken Jin, left and KK Chong right, 1996

With some of my Kembangan Bridge Club players, 2010

TRAVEL

At Marco Polo Bridge, together with Gordon Poon and his wife, and Johnny Fong, extreme left. Nanjing, China, 1980s

La Juanta US Army Air Force Base revisited, Colorado, 2003

With Captain Kirrage (left), Malayan Airways pioneer pilot, me, Mrs Kirrage, Jenny, and Ken Wood and wife. Ken joined Malayan Airways as a radio operator in 1947. London, 1998

Welcome by Gordon Poon and friends at my first visit back to China since leaving in 1949. Beijing, China, 1980

Flying Tigers "Return to China" Tour, Kunming, 1985

At the entrance to the ancient city of Dali, Yunnan, China, 2006

Great Wall, China, 2008

Paris, France, 1982

Los Angeles Olympics, California, USA, 1984

At the Memorial of Resistance to Japan Invasion of China, Nanjing, 2008

Travel

Mongolia, 1990

New York, USA, 1996

Witnessing the new millennium in Queenstown, New Zealand, 2000

Being welcomed by Kasun and some former Chinese Air Force comrades during my first visit to Taiwan in 1965

DOCUMENTS AND LETTERS

I was issued a Kuomintang Passport, which enabled me to travel India and USA for my Air Force training, 1942

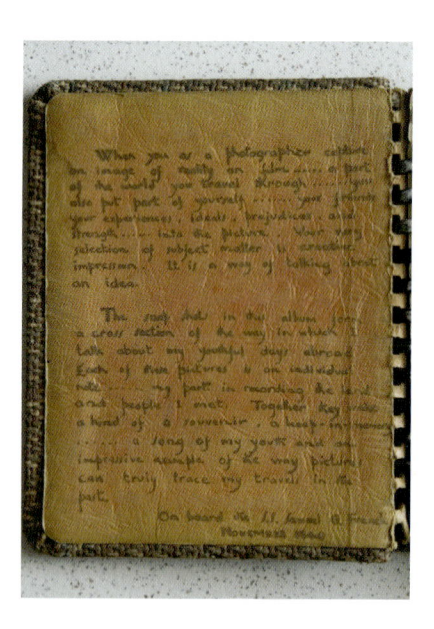

My perspective as a photographer recorded on the first page of my album while sailing back to China, on board the S.S. Samuel G French, 1944

Documents and Letters 305

Details in my Kuomintang Passport, 1942

My pilot logbooks, with Central Air Transport Corporation, left and Chinese Air Force, right

A page from my Chinese Air Force Logbook, China, August 1945

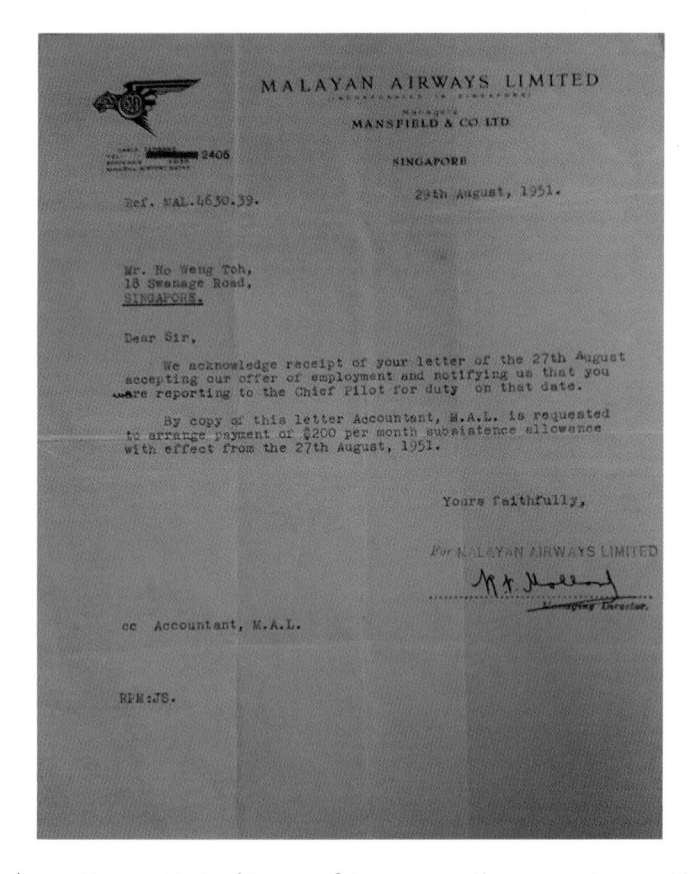

Malayan Airways Limited Letter of Aceptance, Singapore, August 1951

Documents and Letters 307

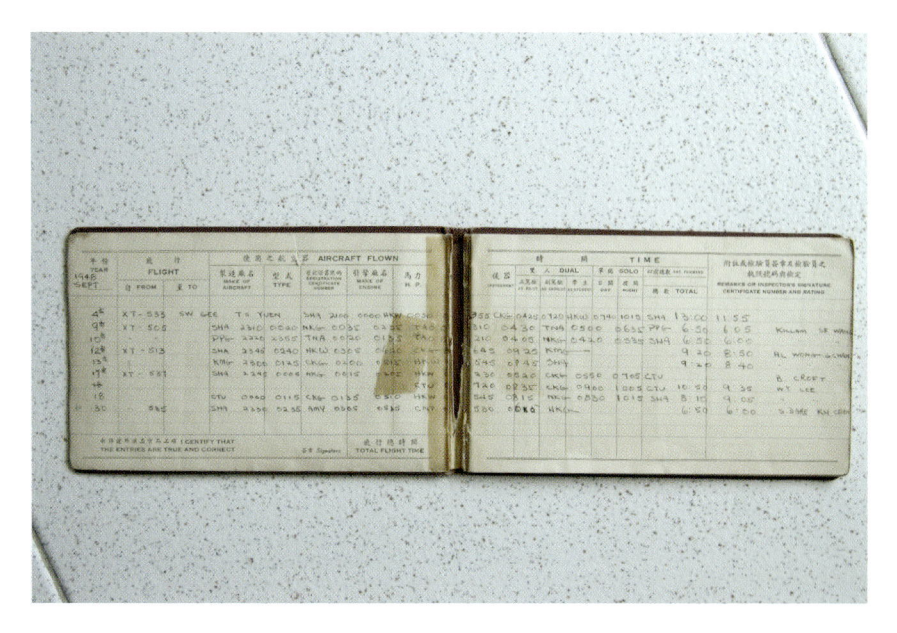

Central Air Transport Corporation Logbook, China, September 1948

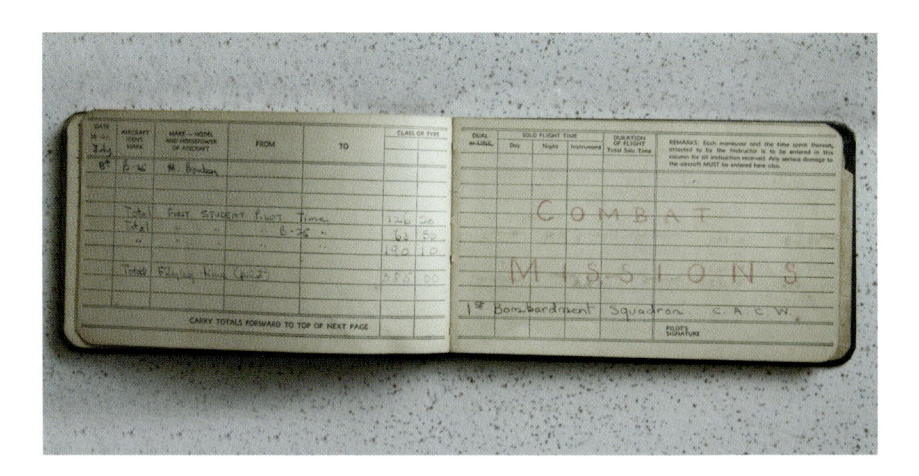

Bombing mission details recorded in my Chinese Air Force Logbook, China, 1944

AWARDS

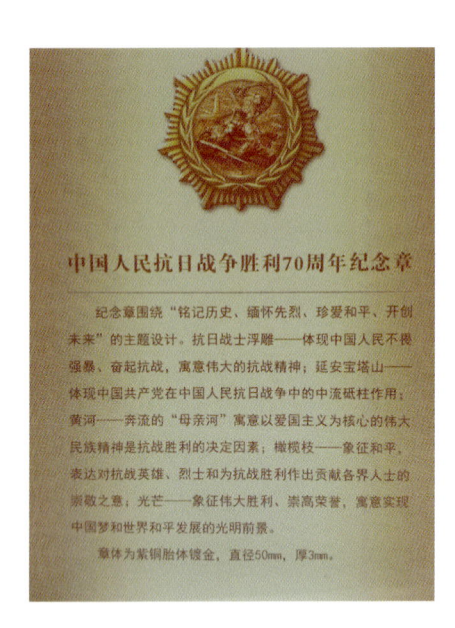

Citation for the 70th Anniversary Commemorative Award for WWII victory over the Japanese, 2015

70th Anniversary Commemorative Medal for WWII victory over the Japanese, 2015

Awards 311

Receiving the Association of Asian Aerospace Professional Award, 2010

Recipient of the Outstanding National Hero Award, presented by the Perak Chinese Assembly, Ipoh, Malaysia, 2015

At 91, I was the oldest recipient of the 2011 Active Agers Award, Singapore